Podemos: In the Name of the People

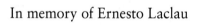
In memory of Ernesto Laclau

Podemos: In the Name of the People

Íñigo Errejón and Chantal Mouffe

A Soundings Publication

Lawrence & Wishart, London 2016

A *Soundings* publication

Lawrence and Wishart Limited
99a Wallis Road
London
E9 5LN

Translated by Sirio Canós Donnay

Foreword © Owen Jones

We gratefully acknowledge the assistance of the Barry Amiel and Norman Melburn Trust for funding this translation.

Sections six and seven were initially translated by Javier Gomez Arribas

First published in Spanish in 2015 by Icaria as *Construir Pueblo*.

ISBN 9781910448 809

British Library Cataloguing in Publication Data.

A catalogue record for this book is available from the British Library

CONTENTS

Acknowledgement

Doreen Massey played a central role in this book. She first suggested that we publish an extract from the Spanish original in *Soundings* (it appears in *Soundings* 62, April 2016), and then, as she was working on it, the idea emerged that we should publish a complete English translation as a *Soundings* publication. When Doreen and I bumped into Sirio Canós at a social event, the book came up in conversation, and Sirio agreed to take on the translation. Doreen, who was fluent in Spanish, then gave us a great deal of detailed useful advice on the text. In discussing this book with Doreen I experienced all the usual pleasures of working with her – her enthusiasm and optimism, her intellectual sharpness, her willingness to get bogged down in technical detail, her pleasure at the emergence of an exciting new political force, and the intertwining of politics and friendship that was so characteristic of her – here with one of her oldest friends, Chantal Mouffe, and one of her newest, Sirio Canós.

Sally Davison April 2016

Preface

Owen Jones

Discontent sweeps the Western world. Across the European continent and the United States, growing numbers are rejecting the existing political order. But this revolt finds two very different political expressions. On the one hand, there has been the growth of progressive movements committed to challenging the concentration of wealth and power in tiny elites, and rejecting policies that expect the majority to pay for the crises of the powerful. On the other, this mass discontent has been funnelled into an altogether more sinister political direction. These political phenomena, unsurprisingly, reflect the political, cultural and historical contexts of each country.

In the United States, for example, the progressive revolt finds its home in the Democratic Party, with a grouchy septuagenarian Senator, Bernie Sanders, becoming the unlikely icon of politicised young people. In Scotland, it was the country's independence movement: when 45 per cent voted to become a separate country in 2014, and the Scottish National Party all but replaced the Scottish Labour Party in the general election a few months later, it wasn't blood-and-soil nationalism at play, but a rejection of a manifestly unjust status quo. In England and Wales – with no tradition, unlike other European nations, of a mass party to the left of social democracy – the Labour Party has proved the vehicle: in the party's 2015 leadership race, the grassroots overwhelmingly rejected the candidates of the party establishment in favour of Jeremy Corbyn, an obscure backbencher who had spent much of his previous political career resisting Tony Blair's New Labour. In Greece, Syriza – standing in the tradition of a Greek left forged in the country's civil war in the 1940s – has proved the beneficiary. And in Spain, of course, Podemos – a party built on the political space created by the indignados, the millions of Spaniards who protested against the old political order from 2011 onwards – is the product of mass political disaffection.

In contrast to all this, in the United States, businessman and reality TV star Donald Trump has become the Republican frontrunner with a platform of toxic demagoguery: banning Muslims from entering the country, and building a wall to keep out Mexican immigrants. His base consists, in part at least, of struggling American workers whose living standards have been squeezed. In Britain, the hard-right UK Independence Party – headed by charismatic former commodity broker Nigel Farage – has surged in support in large part because of its opposition to immigration. France's National Front similarly blames Muslims and immigrants for the country's multiple ills while cynically appropriating the economic rhetoric of the left: and it has achieved record levels of support. Across the Nordic world, far-right anti-immigrant parties like the Swedish Democrats and the Danish People's Party surge. In Greece – a nation ruined by foreign-imposed austerity – the neo-Nazi Golden Dawn have become a political force.

This is the background to the conversation in this book, which explores the political spaces opened up for the left in this new situation.

In part, a crisis in traditional social democracy lies at the root of this polarisation, leaving a vacuum that is being filled by new movements of left and right. Social democracy relied on an alliance of the industrial working class and progressive middle-class people. But this base has fragmented: not least because of a shift towards a more precarious service sector in which communities are not built around workplaces. In the case of Spain, as Íñigo Errejón puts it, this involved 'the dismantlement of the industrial sector and the adaption of our economy to a peripheral role – services, tourism – in the European economy'. A form of globalisation which seemed to curtail the power of national governments, preventing even modest social reform, was another factor. Chantal Mouffe holds parties ostensibly of the left responsible for 'the great surrender to neoliberal hegemony', arguing that they 'accepted the idea that there was no alternative to neoliberal globalisation'. The collapse of the Soviet Union and its satellite states was portrayed as 'the end of history', invalidating any alternative not just to capitalism, but even to the most aggressive, unrestrained form of capitalism. 'What's noteworthy is that social democracy, which you'd think would have gained credibility as a result of this situation, was also discredited', notes Mouffe. 'And along with it was discredited anything related to the fight for equality, assimilated to the Soviet egalitarianism.' Robbed of a traditional base, and with the state (it was argued), deprived of any realistic social-democratic functions, and the end of the Cold War unleashing rampant free-market triumphalism, social democracy shifted dramatically to the right, accepting the essential principles of its supposed neoliberal opponents: privatisation, deregulation, reduced taxation on the rich, and so on. As Chantal Mouffe puts it, 'the best example of the power of the neoliberal hegemony established by Thatcher in Great Britain is the evolution of the Labour Party'.

These factors alone are surely sufficient to plunge social

democracy into crisis: but the social-democratic parties' acceptance (and even implementation) of austerity since the collapse of Lehman Brothers has deepened the malaise of social democracy. If a social democrat no longer even believes in public investment, what is left?

The new movements of the left filling the vacuum face a diverse range of challenges. Class structures and relationships are far more complicated than they once were. The great British marxist historian E.P. Thompson suggested that class wasn't a static concept, but a process: it was about lived experiences, not least about coming into conflict with another class with different interests. But the old industrial era has passed: where communities were once based around factories and mines, they are not typically based around today's supermarkets and call centres. In that male-dominated era, sons might expect to do the same jobs as their father: such generational continuity is far less frequent today. It is now perfectly normal to do two, three, four different jobs in the space of a year; workers may find themselves trapped in a cycle of unemployment and precarious work. Part-time, temporary work and zero-hour contracts have all proliferated, and the phenomenon of self-employment is far more widespread. The workforce has become more fragmented, weakening the organic bonds of solidarity.

But as Mouffe points out, politics depends 'on the creation of an "us" and that necessarily entails the distinction from a "them".' 'To me, the democratic task is not to build a completely inclusive "us" – an us without a them – but to construct the us/them relationship in a way that is compatible with pluralistic democracy.' New Labour claimed that it was capable of surpassing such divisions, its champions describing it as 'the political wing of the British people', and in doing so failed to address the grotesque inequality that scars – and indeed defines – British society. Yet any political project that wishes to transform society must unite the majority of the population, emphasising that they have common, shared interests that are on a collision course with the interests of ruling elites. That means emphasising that whatever differences exist among the majority are far smaller than the differences separating them from those at the top of society. This is by no means straightforward. Across Europe, large swathes of the media, political elites and the populist right have attempted to exploit divisions and tensions. Low-paid workers are encouraged to resent unemployed people; private sector workers are encouraged to resent public sector workers; native workers are encouraged to resent immigrants. A failure to transcend these divisions will simply mean that growing frustrations and resentment will be directed at any target but those with power.

The curtailing of democracy is another challenge. Politicians of centre-left and centre-right stripes have abdicated the responsibilities of elected governments to the market. They preach or plead the limited role of government, reducing the potential power of democracy. 'The most important decisions are taken by unelected powers in a remote sphere that is far removed from any potential control by citizens,' notes Errejón. Rather than politics being a service, with politicians existing to represent the interests of their constituents, the political world has increasingly become professionalised. 'Political representatives resemble each other more and more, and their constituents less and less', as Errejón puts it. In a country such as Britain, the numbers of politicians who have exclusively or predominantly worked in the political world increases with each election. The bad behaviour of politicians – ranging from the 'revolving door' to outright corruption – often perversely undermines the political aspirations of those who believe in far-reaching social change: a widespread response is often to reject politics as a vehicle of change altogether. Politicians treat their ministerial positions as launch pads for lucrative careers in the private sector, cementing a sense of solidarity between the political elite and the corporate world.

One of the other great dilemmas of the left is patriotism. This is an uncomfortable topic for some, who believe it contradicts the left's essentially internationalist mission and regard it as a concession to the right, and to chauvinism or even outright bigotry. But that is not the case with the 'democratic, progressive and popular patriotism' that Errejón refers to; and, as Mouffe says, 'I find it a real problem that the left has a very negative attitude towards the very idea of patriotism, as if patriotism could only manifest itself in reactionary ways.' Those who oppose the status quo are often slighted by its defenders for being 'unpatriotic', as somehow hostile to their own country and its traditions. When Jeremy Corbyn became leader of the Labour Party, the Conservatives instantly labelled the opposition 'a threat to our national security, our economic security, and your family's security.' If the left allows itself to be labelled as such, it is doomed. But Podemos in Spain have been far more savvy, frequently employing the word 'patriotic'. The left should surely argue that there is nothing more patriotic than seeking to rid a country of injustice; of defending the rights and freedoms that our ancestors fought for; or of securing for working people a fair share of the wealth they are creating.

These are disconcerting and uncertain times. The frustrations and insecurities now endemic in European and US society show no signs of dissipating: whether or not there is another economic crisis, they will surely grow. If the left fail to develop an inspiring alternative, a vacuum will be left, and it will be the Donald Trumps, Marine Le Pens and Nigel Farages of the world who will fill it.

Political movements cannot be transplanted into different cultural and political contexts. But Podemos are one of the most intriguing political developments in Western Europe for a long time. Any party that wins the support of millions of people less than two years after being founded is worth studying. In the run-up to Spain's general election in December 2015, I travelled across the country and witnessed rallies of inspired, enthused supporters, brimming with optimism, determined to transform their country. Having grown up in an era of suffocating capitalist triumphalism, it was beyond heartening to see. There are no easy answers for those of us desperate for an alternative to the failed model that currently prevails in the Western world. But Podemos offers clues, and a compelling book such as this is an invaluable resource for those of us determined to build a different society.

1 The project of *Hegemony and Socialist Strategy*

Íñigo Errejón: It's been almost thirty years since, in 1985, you and Ernesto Laclau wrote *Hegemony and Socialist Strategy.* In it you undertake a critical revision of the way of understanding the logic of politics in Marxism – and it is a rich and original reading of Antonio Gramsci's thought. This book has already become, I think you'll agree with me, a foundational text for a school and a theoretical perspective – that of the theory of hegemony – whose analytical fertility makes its current revisiting pertinent. What were the political and intellectual objectives behind its writing? What was your goal? Why did you write it and what did you seek to achieve with it?

Chantal Mouffe: *Hegemony and Socialist Strategy* is a book which is both theoretical and political. The driving force behind it was a political question, at a time when both the social-democratic left and traditional marxism seemed incapable of understanding the specificity of the new movements that had developed since 1968, such as feminism, the environmental movement, anti-racist struggles, and against discrimination on the grounds of sexuality. I was personally involved at the time in the feminist movement in London. I lived through the moment when we were trying to establish connections with the left. The most 'open' would say 'yes, these struggles are very important but not a priority. First we have to establish socialism. The fight against women's subordination will come later'. The least 'open' would say 'these are petty bourgeois demands that move us away from the fundamental struggle'. Therefore, in order to defend what we were proposing as a socialist project, it was important that such a project was defined in a way that could articulate those new struggles.

So, the question was: why was there a disconnect between those new movements and the traditional left? And in discussing that lack of understanding, we realised that the problem was of a theoretical nature: these new fights could not be interpreted in terms of class. This meant that neither marxists nor social democrats could understand them – for although the latter didn't think in terms of class in the marxist way, they still thought in terms of workers' interests. Thus, despite the different theorisation, both currents understood socialism in terms of working-class demands.

What was the obstacle that prevented these groups from understanding the new struggles? In the case of social democracy, it was because they hadn't sufficiently developed these themes; as for marxism, this lack of understanding resulted from their essentialist conception of political identities, which saw them as preceding their discursive articulation. There are many forms of essentialism, and in the case of marxism it was a 'class essentialism', which saw political identities as dependent on the social agent's position in the relations of production, which determined their consciousness.

ÍE: Georg Lukács tries to solve this question with the concepts of 'class in itself' and 'class for itself', by which he distinguishes between belonging and identification, but it is a very unsatisfactory solution, and doesn't quite escape the issue of 'false consciousness'.

CM: Yes, we must acknowledge that there have been attempts inside Marxism to deal with this issue, but they haven't been successful. We believed it was necessary to go beyond that critique. Obviously, we had the advantage over Lukács of living in a time in which post-structuralism was already developing. It was the time when the work of authors like Foucault, Lacan and Derrida was important. We realised there were theoretical tools in that kind of discourse that allowed us to question essentialism, and to produce a notion of the social as a discursive space, the product of contingent political articulations that weren't at all necessary, and could have always been something else.

An important part of the critique of essentialism in political theory has been a questioning of the idea of the subject as a transparent and rational identity, which, being the source of its own actions, can impose a homogeneous meaning across all of its behavioural spectrum. Psychoanalysis, for instance, has demonstrated that, far from being organised around the transparency of an ego, personality is structured at a variety of levels that exist outside the agent's consciousness and rationality. The subject's self-control, a central topic in modern philosophy, is precisely what, according to Freud, can never be achieved. It is from this perspective that our critique of marxist essentialism develops.

ÍE: I find it interesting that you approach this topic from tradition, reviewing all the political thinkers from marxism. It seems to me that there is in the book an uneasiness with the determinist approach that sees politics as a reflection or derivative of social or economic phenomena. You point towards the identification of a particular logic of politics as a meaning-construction activity; and you do so by tracing some of the most fertile ideas within the Marxist tradition, but almost always at their limits, or from, let's say, heterodox or even heretical positions.

CM: Yes, and we also saw how several marxists, for example Rosa Luxemburg, had already attempted to escape that orthodoxy, but had not succeeded.

ÍE: And for those who did succeed, it was by being heretical. Because the best experiences, both theoretical and practical, always ignore the rule books. And such experiences have to be explained in historical terms, because in the end the subject which has achieved a political change, or is in a position to achieve it, is a mixed or amorphous subject – that is, amorphous in terms of class categories. The most productive actions take place at the frontiers, or at the limit: the great revolutions happen where the manuals say it is impossible; and the subjects that lead them are always heterogeneous and diverse blocks articulated around a set of ideas and identifications with an important national or local content.

Let's think about the popular blocs of decolonisation – in China, in Russia itself, or in the heterogeneous societies that have a significant indigenous presence in Latin America, even in Gramsci's obsession with the so-called 'southern question'. There is always the need to build a unity that is not given, either in the economy or in society. It's not question of unveiling something already there, but of articulating differences and forging a collective will.

CM: I agree with you. Post-structuralism gave us a theoretical approach for questioning the basis of essentialism: the specificity of our position was to unite post-structuralism and Gramsci. There were many other groups in the political field who used post-structuralism: in the feminist field, for instance, there was *M/F* journal, with which I collaborated, and which was greatly influenced by the work of Foucault. From such spaces people asserted the importance of feminist and anti-racist struggles. We agreed with them, but also raised something nobody else did: the importance of the concept of hegemony in Gramsci. That led us to assert that it wasn't enough to recognise the existence of a diverse range of struggles, we also had to establish a form of articulation between all those battles. It was an innovative proposal because at the time post-structuralism was very influential, but Gramsci wasn't. The difference with other approaches, such as those influenced by Foucault, was that we argued that to act politically it was necessary to articulate those different struggles with that of the working class, in order to create a collective will. That is *Hegemony and Socialist Strategy's* theoretical specificity: to have brought together Gramsci and post-structuralism.

At the theoretical level, the main categories of our approach are the concepts of 'antagonism' and 'hegemony', which to us are the two necessary concepts for developing a theory of the political. The concept of antagonism is absolutely central, as it states that negativity is constitutive and can never be overcome; and the idea of antagonism also reveals the existence of conflicts for which there is no rational solution. While the concept of hegemony is also key, because to think of the political as an ever-present possibility of antagonism requires acceptance that there is no ultimate foundation, as well as a recognition of the dimension of UNDECIDABILITY and contingency that permeates all order; it requires an acceptance of the hegemonic nature of every social order, and of the fact that all societies are the product of a series of practices aimed at establishing an order in a context of contingency. These are the practices we call hegemonic. All order is the temporary and precarious articulation of contingent practices. Things could have always have been otherwise, and all order is based on the exclusion of other possibilities; it is always the expression of a particular configuration of power relations. What at a given time is considered as the 'natural order', together with the 'common sense' that accompanies it, is always the result of sedimented hegemonic practices; it is never the manifestation of a deeper objectivity external to the practices that make its existence possible. That's why we state that all hegemonic orders can be transformed by counter-hegemonic practices aimed at establishing a different form of hegemony.

At a political level, this analysis led us to a critique of the Jacobin revolutionary model of politics, i.e. a critique of the idea of revolution as a moment of total rupture. We must remember that this was the time when Eurocommunism was influenced by Gramsci's notion that we couldn't think of revolution in the West in the same way it was thought of in the East. That idea was also very important to us, and that's why we suggested visualising the struggle for hegemony in terms of a 'war of position'.

Our main standpoint was that we had to reformulate the 'socialist project' in terms of a radicalisation of democracy. That enabled us to break simultaneously both with the Jacobin tradition and with economic determinism; because you cannot speak about the radicalisation of democracy without recognising that there are different forms of subordination that might give rise to a variety of antagonisms, and that all these struggles cannot be viewed simply as the expression of capitalist exploitation. This is the thesis that is at the core of our political approach in *Hegemony and Socialist Strategy* – and it caused a wide debate in the marxist left.

ÍE: And now, three decades later, after so much has happened in the political and intellectual terrain, when we look at that work and the approach it founded, what evolution do you think it has had, and what are the challenges or difficulties it presents? – because it was a book written to face certain political and theoretical challenges, and today we face challenges of a very different nature. How has that work aged and what revision would you undertake today of the challenges of its approach?

CM: Well, I wouldn't talk about a need for revision. I think the perspective is still valid. It may seem a bit presumptuous, but I believe that events over these thirty years have demonstrated that we were right in stating the need to conceptualise emancipatory politics in a different way. When we published the book we were viciously attacked by all traditional marxists. It's interesting to note that, thirty years later, many of them are no longer marxists, and some have abandoned the fight altogether. There are very few traditional marxists left and those that remain play a marginal role. But the critique of essentialism is still entirely relevant for apprehending the nature of the new struggles that have emerged with the transformations of capitalism and the application of the post-Fordist model. In fact, we could say that the hegemonic perspective is fundamental for understanding what has happened over these thirty years, which have witnessed the decline of social-democratic hegemony and the rise of neoliberal hegemony. When we wrote the book, we were still under a social-democratic hegemony. We were critical of the limits of the welfare state, and of a number of its institutions, but that did not prevent us from recognising the advances it had brought. We argued it is was necessary to go further, to radicalise those advances, and to extend them to a growing number of social relations.

Thirty years later, as the result of neoliberal hegemony, social democracy has now turned into what Stuart Hall called 'a social-democratic variant of neoliberalism'. In a way, we could say that social democracy has self-destructed. Clearly that's what's happened with the Third Way model theorised by Anthony Giddens and put into practice by Tony Blair and New Labour. The prevailing idea became that, with the collapse of the Soviet model, antagonisms had disappeared and there was no alternative to capitalism. Giddens in the UK and Ulrich Beck in Germany defended the thesis that the phase of first modernity and its model of adversarial politics was over; we had entered a second modernity characterised by the disappearance of collective identities and the triumph of individualism. As Tony Blair said, 'we are all middle class now'. According to them, we had to 'rethink progressive politics' in terms of a 'radical centre'.

In those thirty years, two things happened that are key to understanding the current situation: at a political level, there was the development of a vision which I've called 'post-politics', according to which there are no longer antagonisms, so that the adversarial model of politics had thus become obsolete; and, at an economic level, there was the development of a new type of financial capitalism, which created new forms of subordination.

ÍE: And it has also further dislocated and fragmented the social ground, making it even more difficult to think that the political can ever be the faithful expression of something that is already socially constructed.

CM: Yes, we already thought that theorisation in terms of social class, in the marxist way, was inadequate, because social classes are constructed social subjects. But in a way, at the time we could still imagine there were social groups which identified in terms of social classes. Since then, with the transformation of capitalism, things have considerably changed.

I would also like to point out that there were many misunderstandings regarding the political project of *Hegemony and Socialist Strategy*. For instance, a number of people thought that the project of radical and plural democracy that we defended meant a radical break with pluralist democracy. Somehow those people still thought from a Jacobin perspective. I clarified this question in a later book called *Dimensions of Radical Democracy*, where I specified that radical democracy, as we understood it, did not entail a total rupture with pluralist democracy, that it was a radicalisation of the principles of freedom and equality which had already been developed – albeit in a limited and insufficient way – by social democracy.

Another point I'd like to insist on is that I consider left-wing political parties largely responsible for the great surrender to neoliberal hegemony. They accepted the idea that there was no alternative to neoliberal globalisation, that all they could do when they got to power was to manage 'more humanely' the order created by neoliberalism – with a bit more redistribution, for instance. But the hegemony established through neoliberalism was not to be questioned. In fact, the current situation is far worse than it was when we wrote the book, because in 1985 there was still a fundamentally social-democratic common sense that took social rights and the value of equality for granted. With the victory of neoliberal hegemony, that social-democratic common sense has been destroyed, new forms of identity have been created, and people no longer have the same values: there is a new individualism and widespread consumerism. Furthermore, the privatisation policies carried out by both centre-right and centre-left governments have meant that most of the welfare state institutions have been dismantled. Thus, ironically, nowadays we have to defend the social-democratic institutions we previously criticised for not being radical enough. We could have never imagined that the working-class victories of social democracy and the welfare state could be rolled back. In 1985 we said 'we need to radicalise democracy'; now we first need to restore democracy, so we can then radicalise it; the task is far more difficult. There has been a clear regression. But I'm thinking fundamentally from England and France, the countries in which I lived. How has that evolution taken place in Spain?

2 Spain and the transition to democracy

ÍE: In Spain we're currently living through an intense political moment, in which the balances that for over thirty years have ordered a very stable political map are breaking down; they are crumbling as the result of the intersection of a number of different phenomena.

Firstly, I think we should speak of an oligarchic offensive in Spain. That is to say, the thirty-year-old social settlement is being attacked – even broken and violated – not through the rise of popular and democratic forces, making greater demands, but through an offensive from privileged groups, who have been concentrating wealth and power to a greater extent than in the preceding decades, and are therefore disrupting a situation of certainty and settled expectations. It is the elites who have liberated themselves from the existing mechanisms of control, citizen trust, and compromise between groups. They have led a 'de-constituent' drift from the 1978 settlement, which has seen ever more power, income and influence concentrated at the top of the pyramid.[1]

This has coincided with the financial crisis of Spain's precarious productive and social protection system, which has severely hit working-class people, as well as destroying middle-class hopes of social mobility, thus eroding middle-class attachment to their subordinated role within the oligarchy. At the same time, the gap between representatives and the represented has grown wider, leading to what political scientists call 'disaffection' – which at a more popular level can be understood as 'divorce'. This is because political confrontation has been replaced by electoral competition between political machines that operate within the same frame of consensus – which is itself agreed outside the reach of popular sovereignty. But it is also because of the role of corruption as a generalised mechanism connecting the party system with the state and show-business structure in Spain, ensuring the rule of those who do not run for election through a series of networks which have hijacked the institutions. Because of this double phenomenon of ideological rapprochement and corruption, groups within the elite are perceived as cousins, above any of their supposed ideological differences – which are rarely displayed other than in campaign times.

---

1 1978 was the date of the new Spanish Constitution, and widely regarded as a key milestone in the transition from Francoism to liberal democracy, following on from the Moncloa Pacts signed in 1977.

CM: I would first like to know more about how democracy was established in Spain, and the conditions in which it was established. For instance, can we talk about a social-democratic moment in Spain?

ÍE: It was weak, timid. I believe it came into existence during the Transition in the Moncloa Pacts, and later in the Constitutional Pact of 1978, which was the result of a specific correlation of powers. Vázquez Montalbán described it as 'a correlation of weaknesses' – marked on the one hand by the inability of the Francoist oligarchy to continue as usual, and the need to undertake substantive reforms; but on the other hand also marked by the inability of the democratic forces to precipitate a rupture with the previous regime.[2] This incapacity on both sides produced a sort of 'catastrophic tie', as García Linera called it:[3] the leadership of the transition process from dictatorship to parliamentary monarchy was largely comprised of the elites themselves – or, rather, it was drawn from the reformist part of the dictatorship's elites, but with very important participation by the main unions and political organisations of the democratic opposition: unions and left-wing organisations like the Communist Party and the Socialist Party.

This can be understood as a manoeuvre that Gramsci describes in terms of 'passive revolution' and transformism. This refers to a situation when a previously dominant group, no longer capable of continuing with its 'normal'

---

2 Montalbán was a well-known Spanish writer, a political prisoner during the dictatorship, and a member of the Catalan Communist Party (PSUC).

3 García Linera is a Bolivian politician, vice-president of Bolivia since 2006.

handling of things, has to incorporate a large part of the opposition's demands in order to regroup and continue its rule – in Spain essentially those of the workers', students' and neighbourhood movements, which had enough strength to prevent continuity but not enough to precipitate change and a new popular leadership. Change thus came from adjustments in the ruling group's way of ruling, rather than from a new ruling group taking power. In making this move they deprived the opposition both of initiative and of its best leaders and intellectuals, thus safeguarding those of the old leading groups. This was not a matter of deception or treason, but a manoeuvre of extended hegemony restoration – one that oxygenated pluralism and incorporated other social groups to the power bloc, though in a subordinate way. In this way it modified existing institutional and social conditions – incorporating new forms of mediation and new counterbalances, and introducing popular guarantees into the legal order – and forged a narrative and an intelligentsia that solidified the new order. In Spain, this was the hegemony of the Transition.

This situation inaugurated a social and political settlement that has been in place for the last thirty years, under which the popular sectors have access to important benefits, but in a subaltern role within the state. Thus, we reached our own version of the welfare state, a Spanish version, late and weak – or a Mediterranean version, in terms of the analysis of Esping-Andersen. In our case, the welfare state is not dependent on the state's capacity for tax collection: its redistribution mechanism is largely based on European funds.

Clearly, this produced a mechanism for the incorporation of the elites of the popular sectors, left-wing unions and intellectual organisations into the new liberal democratic order. I'd say, however, that in no sense should this be seen as a deceitful manoeuvre, it was compromise between elites – a compromise that left a large part of the previous regime's oligarchic powers untouched, but which also consolidated important advances in the rights of popular sectors. It must be said that this settlement took place after the greatest surge in mobilisation and struggle of Spanish history.

1976 saw the greatest number of strikes and neighbourhood and student mobilisations, as well as an increased capacity for mobilisation and great popular pressure. This mobilisation was strong enough to prevent the dictatorship from continuing without modifications, and to open another political cycle, but not strong enough to lead it and produce a democratic rupture. The 1978 political regime results from this equilibrium and its institutionalisation.

CM: I can see that these developments are very different from those in the UK or France. What is the moment in which neoliberal hegemony becomes established in Spain? In the UK it's very clear, with Thatcher – as it is in France, with the change in political direction of the Mitterrand government from 1983. What was that moment in Spain?

ÍE: I'd say it was the Socialist Party, the PSOE, who to a large extent oversaw the neoliberal shift. This was closely related to Spanish integration into the European Union, and the demands made by the EU at that time. This was the time, for example, when the industrial sector was dismantled and our economy began to adapt itself to a peripheral role – services, tourism – in the European economy; there was a dismantlement of a considerable part of its productive capacity both in public enterprises and the private sector.

In cultural terms, I think two things happened in the 1980s: on the one hand, there was the appearance of the notion, defended by leaders of the Socialist Party, that 'it's OK to get rich' – a shift to the idea of individual social mobility, and the erosion of traditional collective identities, mainly class identity. On the other hand, there was a rise in cultural cynicism, a sort of individual cynicism: what was truly modern was for each individual to mind their own business.

CM: Well, yes, in that sense there is a correspondence with France and the UK …

ÍE: Yes, but in Spain it happened a few years later. And that was a time of profound disaggregation, linked to a disenchantment on the part of a large section of the progressive sector with the ongoing transformations and with the leadership of the Socialist Party – a very unproductive political disenchantment. Probably the last important political battle in which you could see the extent of that disenchantment was in 1986, with the referendum on Spanish membership of NATO, which Felipe González won, the 'Yes' campaign won.[4] González was first against joining, but then went on to champion the 'Yes' campaign. That was probably the last moment, the last gasp, of a decade-long period of conflict and political disenchantment in the 1990s that was almost entirely unproductive. The final breakup between the PSOE and the unions took place during the 1988 general strike, and this marked the beginning of the PSOE's loss of hegemony among the working classes, though it was not expressed electorally until 1993. During this period

4 Felipe González was President of Spain from 1982 to 1996, and General Secretary of PSOE from 1974 to 1997.

the reduction in expectations of social mobility, through work for instance, was offset by the logic of easy money, or work in the construction industry and the finance sector; and by the logic of personal enrichment and a 'get-rich-quick' mentality, according to which, yes, your father may have been a worker, but you, in the late 1990s, even without any skill or profession, or any sense of community, have access to much more credit for consumption, and a belief in the possibility of limitless social mobility and flexibility.

In the meantime, the country's productive structures and the state's fiscal and economic capacities kept getting weaker. This pattern of individual mobility and personal enrichment became generalised, as the bubble grew, and it was also symbolic, proclaiming we had finally reached Europe and become a rich country.

CM: In a way, it seems to me that the Spanish case is closer to the French case than to the British one, as you didn't have a Thatcher.

ÍE: But here, the tasks of economic modernisation, though first initiated by late Francoism and the disarticulation of the historical workers' movement, were led by the Socialist Party, together with that very same workers' movement. This is the process of transformation I was referring to before – the deindustrialisation, the disarticulation of low-income communities, the processes of institutionalisation, patterns of individual social mobility and the consensus culture. What is paradoxical is that, through this operation, the centre-left managed to undermine its own social and cultural bases, giving them away to the paradigm of its former adversary – which is now increasingly less so.

CM: Well, something similar happened in France, for, even though in the first two years of Mitterrand's socialist government there was an attempt to radicalise social democracy, they ended up accepting neoliberalism.

ÍE: It is also similar to the case of the Chilean Socialist Party (PSCH). Sara Motta, in her article on the party's role in constructing consent and disarticulating dissent to neoliberal hegemony in Chile, talks about the CSP as the real force behind Chile's integration into neoliberalism. Moreover, our transition was quite similar to the Chilean transition – it was supervised by a section of the dictatorship's power apparatus.

I think the current situation results from the fact that the economic crisis, the 2008 financial crisis, hit a society in which political identifications were already very weak. People kept voting, but the sense of belonging to traditional parties had already eroded. Even when they maintained high voting rates, votes no longer necessarily corresponded to identification and loyalty: people *voted*, but they no longer *were*. Simultaneously, there has also been a collapse of generational expectations. I think that has played a key role for a whole generation who had been told they were 'the generation that had everything', 'the most prepared generation in history', 'a generation facing much better conditions than its forebears'. That had also justified the many sacrifices made by previous generations, with arguments like 'I'm giving things up now but I'm leaving them as legacy for the next generation'. In reality, all that collapsed, and as a result my generation now finds itself the first in three that is going to be worse off than its parents.

CM: Going back to the previous discussion, I would like to know if something similar happened here to what happened in other parts of Europe after the collapse of communism. If you think in terms of left-wing politics, the key events between the publication of *Hegemony* in 1985 and today have been the fall of the Berlin wall, the fall of the Soviet Union, and the crisis of the Communist model. All of these contributed to the expiry of the model they represented. What is noteworthy about this is that social democracy, which you'd think would have gained credibility as a result of this situation, was also discredited. And along with that, anything related to the fight for equality was discredited – it was assimilated to Soviet egalitarianism. There's no doubt that the abandonment of the total rupture revolutionary model was a positive thing, as it was totally unsuitable for Europe; and it was necessary for the left to recognise the importance of pluralist democracy. But the problem is that many on the left then went completely to the opposite extreme, and accepted a model of politics which is essentially the liberal model. Any notion of antagonism was abandoned, to be replaced by a conception of politics as taking place on a neutral terrain: competitors fight to occupy positions within the state, but once they succeed there is no intention of transforming power relations. Any notion of the social order as hegemonically constructed, as a configuration of power relations, was thus entirely eliminated.

Today there is an urgent need to rethink political struggles. Because the models we currently have don't work. When we think about what models there are on the left, we have either the social-liberalism of the 'centre-left' parties, which essentially follow the liberal model, or a wide range of 'extreme left' groups that have no strategy for winning power. That's why the question of hegemony is so important, because it allows us to think about an alternative to those models.

ÍE: I think what you're saying is very true. There was a point in which the reform-revolution opposition collapsed, as it only worked as an opposition of ideal types. If one model collapses, so does the other. And thus we have two categories which are not helpful for thinking, because the reformists don't reform, and the revolutionaries talk but never do revolutions. So it's an opposition that doesn't explain real phenomena. It would seem that the collapse of one of the poles of this opposition also entails the collapse of any possibility of thinking about the construction of collective interests. That's what you mentioned before in relation to the new challenges raised by *Hegemony*.

At the time, it was written to question those who thought political positions were derived from social positions, and you argued that this wasn't something that could be read off directly, that politics was the construction of the public interest, and therefore a cultural battle. Today, thirty years later, the zeitgeist, or spirit of the age, has shifted so much that the book can be used, from the opposite angle, to defend the idea that there has to be a public interest, despite all the dispersion and fragmentation – or maybe precisely because of them. While it's obvious that the universal doesn't pre-exist politics, if living in a society entails the definition of shared problems, adversaries, and goals, it is necessary to propound universality in order to have a horizon of progress. Thirty years ago, the argument was against essentialism and determinism; today it's against 'weak' postmodernism.

To wind up this part of the discussion – in Spain many jokes have been made about the famous 'end of history', and I believe that, although it is now discredited as a theory, this doesn't mean it hasn't left a mark in the common sense of the age, according to which we live in a period where we can no longer expect great upheavals: it is a time for the mere management of technicalities, and, as you said, electoral competition.

CM: And no alternative ...

ÍE: Sure, within a very closed framework. In other words, there is electoral competition within that framework, but when it comes to the key issues, these are decided in advance, in forums beyond the reach of popular sovereignty; and precisely inasmuch as they are presented as 'technical', they cannot be argued with by ordinary people. For us, this 'end of history' was the story of the transition to democracy – which is also very generationally loaded.

Some people today get very nervous at the slightest mention of the fact that we live in a regime that was born in 1978 – with specific contours (democratic-liberal), but born, like any other regime, from pressures, relinquishments and exclusions. And notice I'm not talking here about any proposed historiographical revision, just about the possibility of brushing away some of the cobwebs of praise for the impeccable democratic lesson of the Spanish people – as the official narrative goes – in order to ask questions about its current performance, its difficulties, the blockages that prevent it from responding to some of the needs and aspirations of today's Spain. I think there is a very strong generational identification here, that not only has become official history but has also attempted to close down political development, and the possibility of innovation and forward thinking.

Their story would go: 'We made history and that was the time of great epics. Now that's already been done. Go back home. Study a lot, get rich, and have fun on the weekends.

The time of collective feats is over'. 'We did the best we could'. 'We've already been heroes, we ran in front of Franco's police. The time of collective hopes is over'. And yet, no society can stay healthy without communal goals and hopes.

CM: To me democracy requires the existence of projects you can identify yourself with, and the conviction that there are alternatives worth fighting for.

ÍE: Today I think this generational political imagination, its actors, and its corresponding distribution of positions, are in crisis in Spain. But they are not in crisis because people have undertaken a critical revision of what happened – I don't think many people would be interested in such critique, and is not very productive in political terms either. (Quite possibly we will at some point have to start a historiographical discussion, but I don't think revised forms of nostalgia – let's say, moving away from the melancholy of the loser – is ever productive.) They are in crisis because their myths, actors and institutions are not sufficiently capable of responding to the demands of a large part of the dissatisfied sectors of Spanish society – not because they were not useful in their time, but because they cannot now incorporate this discontent and provide institutional answers. To the extent that this discontent has been building up outside the most important and representative institutions, it has also been building up outside existing political identities, and outside the narrative channels that existed to integrate it, or to order it. A large cache of unattached and fragmented discontent gradually built up.

3. Rethinking the political

CM: That's a question which we must discuss, as I'm convinced that it is only in that context that we can we understand the growing success of right-wing populism. But before getting to that, I think it's worth emphasising the fact that we agree that if we don't want to accept either social-liberalism or the Jacobin model, we must rethink the political.

ÍE: Or the other way round: without rethinking it there is no alternative, because you're caught between cynicism and nostalgia for the centrality of the lost class – yesterday the working class, today the multitude – searching for a social subject which is both pure and represents the possibility of transformation. Between those two cliffs of determinism and cynicism, the possibility of thinking a counter-hegemonic construction dies. Either this possibility is killed off by a religious approach to politics, based on dividing the pure from the traitors, while reciting revolutionary psalms; or subaltern groups are condemned to impotence and dispersion because they are conceptualised as a solitary individuals, without any reference points – celebrated as freedom.

CM: In *Hegemony*, we discussed that new form of politics, and that's why I think the book is still relevant, even when taking into account how much the situation has changed, and that we are not facing the same context or the same challenge. But the central tenet we defended in *Hegemony*, that antagonism and hegemony are the two key concepts for an understanding of the political, is still valid. Against the current tendency to favour consensus, we must recognise that society is divided.

ÍE: Which is also a guarantee of freedom.

CM: Yes, you could say that. That's what Machiavelli said.

ÍE: That society is never completely closed is a guarantee that everything can be questioned.

CM: That's true, because the notion that we could reach a rational agreement in politics is potentially totalitarian, because it would mean that such an agreement could not be questioned.

ÍE: Exactly – that history would end. Also, the idea of antagonism is the basis of an idea that you have developed, of a strong conception of democracy. Democracy is not about everybody agreeing, but about building the procedures and mechanisms which allow for a never-ending dispute over the broadest possible range of topics. A never-ending dispute for establishing the distribution of collective assets and positions. I'm saying this now because yesterday, partly joking, we talked about the idea that in Spain we've reached a point at which democracy, consensus and Constitution appear to be synonymous. When in actuality, democracy is the possibility of choosing between different options, and is strengthened, not weakened, by conflict.

CM: In relation to the question 'what is the political?' there are two fundamental conceptions: one which could be called the associative approach, according to which the political is a space of freedom and public deliberation where we act jointly; while the other is the dissociative approach, in which the political is a space of power, conflict and antagonism. Depending on whether the departure point is an associative or a dissociative approach, problems will be addressed differently. I, evidently, subscribe to the dissociative approach. It's precisely to highlight this that I distinguish between 'the political' – referring to the dimension of antagonism, inherent to human societies – and 'politics' – or the ensemble of practices and institutions that attempt to establish an order, to organise human coexistence in the context of the conflicts generated by 'the political'. What that distinction highlights is, firstly, that the political cannot be reduced to a given place in society, and is not limited to specific institutions, but is, rather, itself a constitutive dimension of social order. And, secondly, that such order is the result of power relations and always contingent, given that it is riddled with antagonisms.

ÍE: The position, typically liberal, that wants to see politics as rational association and maximisation of individual gains, has had to repeatedly face the resurgence of things it thought it could write off – as has been the case with nationalisms, or ethnic identities, for instance, in the face of each 'capricious' revival of the communal. Thinking that differences, disputes and conflicts could be eradicated, it built theories and institutions that closed off channels for the expression of conflict; but these, being ineradicable, have often then appeared outside of, and against, the constituted powers. What's more, from an ethical point of view, only the pain that is named can be confronted and solved. The privileged tend to label as 'disorder' anything that questions their privileges.

In fact, even in emancipatory thought, the most productive ideas have lived in tension with this idea of politics as its own logic – and have recognised this more or less explicitly – at the boundaries or limits of the manuals. That's why I'm interested in 'post' marxism, which isn't an 'anti', but a theoretical perspective located inside an emancipatory matrix but not bounded in its thinking.

CM: Yes, that's very important to us.

ÍE: It's very important to reclaim that heretical tradition, because all those who have been important in building power for the impoverished or for mistreated majorities have done so by breaking with dogma. Not for the sake of iconoclastic posturing, but because the task is always to build a people, a general will, from the pain of the subaltern groups, who don't necessarily have a common 'essence' – sometimes it's just a question of common opposition to the status quo and the dominators – and the hope in a better future. It is never a matter of expressing or revealing, it's always one of weaving, conversing, articulating, calling. We must remember that the experience of the Russian revolution, for instance, was an experience that challenged all the manuals. So are those of Cuba, Vietnam, and China, to cite some of this school's milestones.

4. Gramsci

CM: Remember Gramsci talked about 'The Revolution against "Capital"', seeing in the Russian revolution an act of innovation and daring against the canons, including those of his own school of thought. In relation to Gramsci, I have to admit that the use we make of his ideas in *Hegemony* is slightly heter-odox. For instance, we retrieve his idea of 'war of position', about the struggle inside the institutions, which Gramsci saw as the preparation for the 'war of manoeuvre', the time of revolutionary rupture. But we left the 'war of manoeuvre' one out. Not in the sense that there won't be any kind of rupture, but because the counter-hegemonic struggle is a process involving a multiplicity of ruptures, to disarticulate the many nodal points around which the existing hegemony is struc-tured. Another example: Gramsci says that the central core of a hegemony must always be a fundamental class, and that's something else we dropped. Honestly, I don't think that in doing so we were unfaithful to Gramsci. In fact I'm convinced that if Gramsci had lived in our times, he would have reached a similar conception to ours.

ÍE: He would have. It's impossible to prove, but I've also thought that many times.

CM: Because Gramsci paid a lot of attention to the plurality of currents of thought.

ÍE: His own discussion with Benedetto Croce shows the extent to which he was hungry for traditions from other places.

CM: Yes, and his interest in pragmatism and William James, for instance, shows he was an extremely open person. He thought from a specific context, but I think we have developed Gramsci's thought rather than betrayed it, as some people claim.

There's something which is both fundamental and very heterodox in his approach: he says that the subjects are collective wills, rather than social classes. That's because he is thinking from the Italian context: there's the workers in the north, but also the popular classes and the peasants in the south, and he is aware that a socialist project has to be the articulation of a collective will for these different groups. He talks about the need to think in terms of historical blocs, and that I think is very important to us.

In politics there is a dimension of antagonism, which it is impossible to eliminate, but there is also a need for forms of consensus. In order to establish a hegemony it is necessary to articulate these different groups and to create a collective will among them. Politics has to do with collective subjects. This is something liberals don't recognise and which I think is fundamental.

Collective wills crystallise around a conception of the common good around a definition of public interest, and this is a very important dimension of democratic politics. This could seem paradoxical, given that, according to the pluralist approach I'm defending, the common good doesn't exist because there can be no such thing as 'the' common good. But it plays the role of a horizon. A people is built from a given idea of the common good In other words, there will always be a struggle around the definition of the common good. The fight which I call agonistic is a fight for defining the common good. Those capable of persuading the majority to identify itself with their conception of the common good achieve hegemony. That's why the democratic struggle requires a reference to the common good, while at the same time recognising that there is no such thing as 'the' common good.

ÍE: That it isn't set.

CM: No, I'd say rather that it can't be set.

ÍE: Well, for a while it can, but in a precarious form.

CM: Yes, but it will always be a hegemonic conception.

ÍE: Of course. It isn't natural. But for a while a group is capable of establishing a general interest within a society.

CM: True, but it's always a particular conception that has managed to present itself as universal, and which can be questioned through a counter-hegemonic struggle.

5. Hegemony and the war of position

ÍE: We now come to the concept of hegemony, which is at the heart of this discussion and of this theoretical approach. Here I would distinguish three elements or levels of definition: the incarnation of the universal as the particular; the capacity for persuasion and creation of consent; and the construction of the very terrain on which the dispute takes place.

In the first instance, as you mentioned earlier, there is the capacity of a particular sector to construct itself as the public interest for a given period, in what is in a certain sense an arbitrary way, in the sense that it isn't predetermined.

CM: I would prefer to say contingent. Because it's never really arbitrary, it always exists within a particular context.

ÍE: Yes, in your terms, contingent. It always involves an exclusion: it could have been decided otherwise, but it has been decided like this. That metonymic substitution, always precarious and contested, makes it possible for a part to represent the whole. For a while, the particular interest coincides with the general development of society. The development of a group appears to be in step with the general development of society, which means that this group can speak in society's name, attach its own labels to things, and define themes and adversaries. This is the first element.

The second element addresses a key question for anybody who wants to change things: why are those in power in power? Our societies are ruled by those capable of constructing a general consent for their leadership, and of making people see the world through their eyes, and with their language and concepts. This relationship of consent is very specific because it's unstable and always negotiated. In other words, it needs to integrate some of the subordinates' needs, while removing their character of total contestation. That, I think, is key for any possibility of thinking about change, for otherwise one gets stuck in the impotence of thoughts like 'those in power are in power, and that's it'. We need to realise that those in power are in power because they have the ability both to integrate and exclude. The ways of thinking of the dominators always include, in a subordinate form, those of the dominated: they give them meaning, and some form of hope within their order. Coercion is thus always the *ultima ratio*.

This always reminds me of a remark made by Nicos Poulantzas, who said, in a different context, 'the capitalist state always has the mission of aggregating at the top and dispersing at the bottom, that is, to fragment and disperse discontent'. The state integrates some of the discontent, and condemns the rest to resignation and marginality.

The third element to look at is the way in which hegemonic power is the kind of power that, even when it is being defied by its adversaries, must be defied in its own terms. In other words, it is a power that constructs the playing field, that constructs common sense, and that forces anybody attempting to defeat it to do so in its own political ground. Jaime Guzmán, one of the architects of the post-Pinochet Chilean Constitution, said: 'this is about creating a Constitution such that, should an adversary win, he would have to govern in a very similar way to ours'. Another extremely clear example is Margaret Thatcher's response when asked what she regarded as her greatest achievement. She replied, without hesitation: 'Tony Blair and New Labour. We forced our opponents to change their minds'.

CM: Unfortunately she was right. The best example of the power of the neoliberal hegemony established by Thatcher in Great Britain is the evolution of the Labour Party under Tony Blair. When Labour reached power, they accepted the neoliberal hegemony. Under the pretext of modernisation, they rejected the 'Old Labour' values, without any attempt to undertake a counter-hegemonic fight to transform power relations. That's why neoliberalism is still hegemonic in Great Britain.

ÍE: In this sense I think your approach is excellent, because counter-hegemony is not a complete rejection, or a total exteriority. It accepts part of the hegemonic order and aims to rearticulate it and give it a sense of contestation: it has one foot in the existing common sense, and the other in the possibility of change.

CM: That's what Gramsci calls a war of position. It's a strategy of disarticulation/re-articulation. This is an idea which I think is crucial.

ÍE: It's not a frontal collision but rather a system of warfare based on a fortresses and earthworks, as he describes it.

CM: Gramsci insists on the importance of struggle in the field of culture, because to a large extent that's where common sense is built, and it's also in the cultural field where one can subvert it. That's why I'm interested in artistic and cultural practices, and on how they could contribute to counter-hegemonic struggles.

ÍE: In the political experience of Podemos, here and now, we have the example of our political intervention on TV, which, while it's not a comparable field, is one in which the same logic operates. It's a field clearly built by the adversary, and with the adversary's logic and ways of thinking and expression. I would prefer to face my adversaries in a format like the conversation we are having now. I don't think it's unreasonable to say that I would do well in that kind of format. I would much prefer that to having to shout, in very short and shallow formats. Clearly, that's a playing field built by the opponent, but at the same time, in order to maintain its legitimacy it has to incorporate new voices like ours. It has had to incorporate other voices because there's been a shift in attitudes that has generated a hunger for new voices, and by incorporating them it has also opened a space for dispute.

And it's true, of course we're fighting on a terrain built by the adversary, because the opponent is hegemonic; but it's possible to fight in and against, or on the inside but trying to cut across that setting to give it a different meaning. And I think that's the crux of the matter, the key to counter-hegemony: to be capable of operating from within and from outside at the same time, or from within and cutting across.

CM: To be able to address the possibility of counter-hegemonic struggle it is necessary to understand that there is no natural order, that all orders are constructed by an articulation of power relations; in other words, that they are the product of a series of practices which in *Hegemony* we called hegemonic. That's why any order is hegemonic, because it excludes other possible power configurations which could always be reactivated through a counter-hegemonic struggle.

ÍE: And all orders try to naturalise themselves. Even though they are not natural, they try to erase their traces, their borders, to appear as the only possibility, to make people forget that at their birth there were, inevitably, decisions, exclusions and violence; or that the existence of any order is always temporary and unstable, because to sustain itself it must negotiate its contradictions and thus open cracks or include new contents. That makes politics a risky and uncertain sport, but it also makes it sometimes possible for the humble to win.

CM: Yes. In order to establish itself, any order has to leave aside other alternatives. But there are always alternatives. That philosophical-theoretical perspective is very important for thinking about politics. If you accept that there are always alternatives, that means those alternatives can be reactivated. That's what makes a counter-hegemonic struggle possible, the strategy of disarticulation-rearticulation which characterises the war of position we discussed earlier on.

ÍE: Of course, there are always alternatives. Besides, the very form in which ruling sectors build their hegemony always opens cracks or loopholes which can be used for intervention in a counter-hegemonic direction. It is not only a matter of resolution, it cannot always be done, but there are situations – and we'll talk about that later – as in the Spanish case, where there is a hegemonic crisis: those in power still rule, but they no longer convince. They are no longer capable of offering a project for the country that includes the majority of the population, not even in subordinate form; they can no longer construct a public interest satisfactorily enough to bring everybody together. That opens certain political possibilities that a more static and essentialist view of politics cannot see or smell. It seems to me that to see those possibilities it's necessary to embrace a form of understanding politics that recognises positions are not given but constructed.

CM: I completely agree. That's why I always insist on the importance of theoretical reflection for political praxis. Over the years, I've had several opportunities to argue about this with Richard Rorty, who claimed politics was a 'banal' activity, a simple matter of implementing reforms which didn't require any theory, only a good dose of tolerance.

ÍE: After the European elections in May 2014, we were very often asked: 'what's the magic formula by which, without money or membership, so soon after being born, you've obtained a 1.25 million votes?'

And of course, this was hard to say as it could sound arrogant, but our response was that it was necessary to study. We couldn't go on with an approach to politics that believed that the graphs showing the distribution of MPs and seats defined what was possible. A type of politics that at the most said 'what I want is to unite the left, so if we look at this piece of the pie here, which is 6 per cent, let's see if we can add in this and add in that, and lump it all together to make 6 per cent'.

An anti-essentialist and hegemonic view of politics allowed us to understand that there were conditions which couldn't be seen with the naked eye but nevertheless existed. These were not certainties, but potentialities for an intervention that could draw a border and start building a new popular majority for rupture. The organic crisis of the 1978 regime – not to be mistaken for a state crisis – and the rise of the 15M opened new possibilities for counter-hegemony and the postulation of a new people.

CM: Yes, precisely. If you hadn't had that alternative view, if you had thought from a different theoretical perspective, you couldn't even have considered such an intervention. Because if you're limited to the liberal view of competition between interests, or to the Bolshevik view, you can't conceive a strategy like that of Podemos.

ÍE: And neither can you from the 'escaping the state' view, the idea of the autonomous area, a road along which some of us have travelled. This view stated – maybe it still does – that 'the social' is the privileged site from which to build: it is primordial, it precedes the institutional – and of course the mercantile. It is an unpolluted terrain from which the construction of popular power should start. When we launched the idea of Podemos, many people told us, based on this social determinism, that we were putting the cart before the horse. As if an election, or the dispute of institutional politics, could not build popular identification. In our case, anyway, it was not an ideological or static choice, but a strategic one: we took advantage of a window of political opportunity, a situation which the transformative sectors had arrived at with some options, but also with many weaknesses and deficiencies – after all, the tempo is seldom to the taste of those who are defying the existing order.

CM: That exodus strategy is still in vogue amongst many activist groups. It seems very radical, but actually can be seen as a postmodern form of traditional marxism. In the end, what Negri and Hardt defend is a new version, a more sophisticated one, of the Second International's determinism, but now using a vocabulary influenced by Deleuze and Guattari. They talk about 'the multitude' instead of the proletariat, but it is still a sort of economic determinism. At the core of their reflection is the thesis that the transformations of capitalism connected to the transition to post-fordism have brought into being an entirely new epoch. In 'cognitive' capitalism, the central role in the production of surplus value – previously played by the labour power of the industrial mass worker – is now filled by the power of immaterial work, of the intellectual and communicative type. That's why they use a new term, 'the multitude', to refer to the figure of the immaterial collective worker.

This multitude has to tackle the Empire of globalised and de-territorialised capitalism, which has no territorial centre or fixed borders. Hardt and Negri claim that with the development of cognitive capitalism, the role of capitalists has become parasitic, and that they will eventually disappear as a result of the increase of the multitude's power. This optimistic view explains why, from their perspective, it's not necessary to attempt to transform the existing institutions: they are bound to disappear anyway. That's why the exodus strategy they propose is a 'desertion' strategy, one of abandonment of the traditional centres of power to establish places outside them, where the multitude can self-organise and enjoy the exercise of 'the common'. They say that the multitude's democracy expresses itself through a set of active minorities which never aspire to turn into a majority, but instead develop a power that rejects becoming a government. Their way of being consists in 'acting in concert' and refusing to become a state. Hardt says there are three ways of approaching the concept of multitude: at an economic level, the multitude opposes the working class; at a philosophical one it opposes the People; and at the political level it opposes the party. It's true that more recently they've slightly moderated their ideas. They now say, for instance, that they are not against the state. But I don't see how their recent statements can be compatible with their general approach.

ÍE: They also describe spaces which I've seen in other societies but which don't exist in Western ones. They have a sort of romantic fascination – I'm not sure if you'll agree with me here – which is also a bit liberal, with that division between the social and the political. They describe a social ground unpolluted by the market and the state, which I have never seen in the so-called First World. There are no citizens of that world living in spaces which haven't been captured and regulated by the logic of the market or the state. Yes, there were some in El Alto, in Bolivia, or in micro-spaces like the Zapatista communities, but not in our case. Thus, there is no such thing as the 'outside' of the institutional; and that separation between the social and the political – which to me has always seemed liberal – does not exist either.

This takes us to a question which was very controversial when we launched Podemos. Amongst a substantial part of the transformative or progressive sectors there's the idea – now I think on the wane – that the social comes before the political, and that to start with a political construction, even more so if it's an electoral one, is to put the cart before the horse. You first have to build a social force, and only then can you run for election, if you wish to do so. Like the person that goes to the casino counter to exchange money for chips or chips for money. 'Look, I have this many chips of social force, how many votes or seats does that give me?' And they exchange them for you.

This is connected to a mistaken reading of the Latin-American experiences, according to which there has been a linear accumulation of power by social movements that has then gone to the polls. This has led to the formation of governments, which of course, like all governments, have betrayed the movement, always more beautiful in its never realised potential.

In actuality, this is not true: in the majority of cases, the mobilisations were either receding or had not accumulated enough power – or if they had, it was more destituent than constituent.[5] As I think is the case with us, it was electoral competition which started to produce a bond and a new political identity, around new leaders and symbols, thus defying first social determinism, and then political. There is no social which hasn't been built by the political.

CM: I agree, the social is always built through the political. One of the theses we developed in *Hegemony* is that all societies are the product of a series of practices attempting to establish order in a contingent context. These acts of hegemonic institution are of a political nature. It is in that sense that we can distinguish the social from the political. The social

5 Destituent is a term more commonly used in Spanish and Italian than in English. According to Giorgio Agamben: 'Whereas constituent power seeks to resume and reform the law, destituent power seeks to render it inoperable'. In other words destituent is the opposite of constituent.

is the field of sedimented practices; that is to say, practices that obscure the original acts of their contingent political institution and are taken for granted, as if they substantiated themselves. We insist that power is constitutive of the social, because the social could not exist without the power relations that give shape to it. That which at any given time is considered as 'natural' – together with the 'common sense' that goes with it – is always the result of sedimented hegemonic practices, never a manifestation of a deeper objectivity, external to the practices that produce it. That's why society shouldn't be perceived in terms of the deployment of a logic which is external to it, regardless of the supposed origin of this logic: whether it's Marx's productive forces, Hegel's development of the Absolute Spirit, or the laws of history of the several positivist currents.

This conception of the social is fundamental, as it makes it possible to imagine how a given order can be transformed. But there is another question which is important for understanding the hegemonic struggle, and on which I think we agree. It's the fact that political identities are always collective identities. That's something marxism does understand, but it thinks about it only in terms of class. Marxism also understands the idea of antagonism, but the problem is that it thinks there is only one form of antagonism, class, which cannot be eliminated. We, on the other hand, maintain that there are several types of antagonism, and that there cannot be a society where the possibility of antagonism has been eradicated. There is a radical negativity, which can never be overcome, and society is thus always divided.

We must recognise that marxism at least acknowledges antagonism and collective identities. In the case of liberalism, you cannot find any sense either of antagonism or collective identities. But neither perspective allows us to understand the nature of politics.

ÍE: It is true that in marxism collective identities have an important weight, but they can still be 'true' or 'false' depending on whether they reveal or obscure the reality of the subjects in the productive system. This makes it possible to classify identifications morally, but not to explain or modify them. Solidarity and the ties constructed in an identification appear as the result of other forces, instead resulting from conscious and changing activity, and as the crucial moment of the political.

CM: Yes, the famous theory of false consciousness.

ÍE: Exactly – the false consciousness that sometimes also manifests itself in national constructions. In Spain, for instance, in the dominant national story – the Spanish one – peripheral national identities, whether Basque or Catalan, are often accused of being false. Well, let's see: if you have millions of citizens on the streets identifying themselves as belonging to the same nation, that's precisely the definition of a nation. There was an old trade unionist here in Spain, a social democrat, who said: 'there is nothing more foolish than a right-wing worker'. Saying this is morally reassuring but it doesn't explain why it happens, and why it happens to so many millions. Why does this happen? To say they have false consciousness is to condemn them from an aristocratic position. It's like saying 'they haven't understood a thing, unlike me, that's why they don't pay attention to what I say'. These reflections do not explain what sort of cultural warfare has been able to produce the identifications by means of which somebody with a worker's salary votes as if they were the owner of a second home, for instance. Or votes against the migrant, rather than against the owner of a business. Of course, the idea of false consciousness can give moral validity or invalidity, but it doesn't explain anything. It doesn't help us to understand why. '*Eppur si muove*' [And yet it moves]. In politics, the positions and the ground are not given; they are the result of the battle for meaning.

6. Carl Schmitt, antagonism and agonism

CM: To me, a decisive element for thinking democratic politics is the recognition that while antagonism is ineradicable, the existence of a pluralist democracy is possible. Somebody who it would be interesting to introduce into the discussion here is Carl Schmitt, who to me has been both a source of inspiration and a constant challenge.

ÍE: Yes, I discovered him thanks to you.

CM: Schmitt insists on the importance of antagonism. That's why his critique of liberalism is so powerful. He says that in denying the ineradicable character of antagonism, liberalism is incapable of apprehending the nature of 'the political', which is characterised by the discrimination between friend and enemy – which requires the formation of an 'us' as opposed to a 'them', both of which are always collective subjects. This is something that necessarily escapes liberalism and its individualist perspective. The dimension of 'the political' has to do with conflict and antagonism, and constitutes therefore a sphere of decision, not one of free discussion. If there is politics in society, it is because of the dimension of conflict that exists in all human societies. On that point I find a convergence with Freud's reflection on Eros and Thanatos, and the impossibility of a final harmony. Freud and Schmitt come from different traditions – though there's a common reference to Hobbes – but both are important to my thinking.

In the case of Schmitt, I've said that to me he represents a challenge because, while I agree with his conception of the political as discrimination between friend and enemy, I don't accept his rejection of pluralist liberal democracy. He says it's an unviable regime because liberalism denies democracy and democracy denies liberalism. It's not possible to acknowledge pluralism, and to accept conflict, inside a political association, because that would take us, he says, to civil war, and thus it's a type of conflict which cannot be considered legitimate.

ÍE: Or at least not all the time – there are always foundational moments characterised by this rise of passion and the resort to the *ultima ratio* of politics, which is warfare; and it is precisely to channel those conflicts that we build institutional pluralist systems.

CM: Yes, but in the normal development of democracy we cannot accept as legitimate parties whose goal is to eradicate their opponents. That's why, if one believes, as is the case with Schmitt, that the only way antagonism manifests itself is in the friend/enemy form, one must conclude that the recognition of antagonism isn't compatible with pluralist democracy. This idea is actually quite similar to some found on the liberal side. They agree with Schmitt on the fact that antagonism cannot coexist with pluralist democracy and that's why they deny the existence of truly antagonistic conflicts, i.e. those without a rational solution. I'm thinking for instance of Habermas, who claims that the recognition of antagonism undermines democracy. So if we are to accept that antagonism is an ineradicable dimension, but also want to defend the possibility of a pluralistic democracy, we must find a way of responding to Schmitt.

That's what I've been trying to do in my work, and that has led me to think with Schmitt, as well as against him, as I base myself on Schmittian premises to reach an approach contrary to his in terms of the possibility of a pluralist democracy.

ÍE: The best part of what you've rescued from Schmitt's thought is, in my view, the understanding of politics as encompassing an intensity that can inhere in any type of relation and any subject that involves the establishment of a friend-enemy relationship. This intensity and friend-enemy relationship are always a political matter, and this provides an approach to politics which I think is both flexible and agile. It doesn't view politics only through institutions or elections, but also as an activity that chooses, from among many options, the axes and topics that define a society's alignments and positions. Because these can greatly vary, politics cannot be seen as an already defined chessboard, where you start with one opponent on each side and advance from there. No, you can redraw the board, not freely, but you can try. The 'raw materials' to build meaning and political aggregation are given by a sum of present and sedimented factors. But the meaning that these might take on, and the direction of their policitisation – the conflict that might be created around them – is not.

CM: Yes, for Schmitt 'the political' isn't located in a particular area of society, it's something that can manifest itself in a multiplicity of social relations.

ÍE: We caused quite an uproar here when we said we wanted to occupy 'the centre of the board'. There was a general interpretation that led many to think: 'these people have become centrists'. But we said 'no, not at all, what we're saying is that it's possible to reorder and redraw the existing positions by establishing new borders, and redefining who occupies what position: so – is it centrist to evict families?' Because politics is the production of identities, a grouping together around shared interests and projects, a disaggregated and fragmented discontent like the one we had here opened the door to the creation of a different border, capable of producing new identities – identities which, like the ones you've worked on, always express an 'us and them'. There's always the denomination of a 'them' against which the 'us' is constituted. This has been crucial for the possibility of aggregating the existing discontent-resignation into an incipient desire for a different type of power, for change. Something that has been decisive in the construction of a people and its political direction is the 'anti-people', the adversary that marks the impossibility of what is currently perceived as legitimate. In our case, that meant pointing to the evident oligarchic evolution: the *casta*, the privileged.[6]

CM: It's crucial to understand that politics consists of the creation of an 'us', and that necessarily entails the distinction from a 'them'. To me, the democratic task is not to build a completely inclusive 'us' – an us without a them – but to construct the us/them relationship in a way that is compatible with pluralistic democracy. That us/them relation is not

6 *Casta* is Spanish for 'caste', and it has become a key part of the vocabulary of Podemos.

the expression of something already existing, of an essentialist nature, but always results from a discursive construction. I think some of those constructions go against pluralist democracy, but there are others which, on the contrary, can be key to reinvigorating it.

All of this depends on how you build the frontier, and that's precisely what I've tried to explore in my proposal of agonistic democracy.

My proposal is based on the acknowledgement of antagonism and its ineradicability, but I also state that antagonism can manifest itself in two ways: in friend-enemy form, or as what I call 'agonism', which takes place between 'adversaries'. The latter is a sublimated form of the antagonistic relation, in which the opponents know there is no rational solution to their conflict and that they'll never be able to agree, but accept the legitimacy of the adversaries in defending their position. This requires the availability of institutions capable of channelling conflict into an agonistic, rather than antagonistic form. In both cases there is a frontier, but it's constructed differently.

ÍE: There is a very common criticism to this, vaguely drawing from liberalism, which says: 'why such need to divide? why do you want to divide people between us and them? isn't it easier to be all part of the same thing? I think this is a critique that forgets, firstly, that there is an asymmetrical distribution of wealth and social benefits; and secondly, that the pain does not disappear if it's not named. To name it is the best way of facilitating its incorporation into the public agenda. The majority of those who see 'aggressiveness' in naming the pain, tend to forget there is actual pain behind the numbers.

In any case, this criticism always forgets that all identifications that motivate people always have a 'constitutive outside'.

Nobody ever displays with euphoria the flag of the United Nations or the white flag, because they don't represent something with an outside; and since they represent something without an outside, they cannot define an inside. All identities need a difference that is postulated as paramount, and politics feeds from the mobilised affection of the us/them clash.

CM: I have a philosophical response to that point, but it might be too complex to be explained in detail here. When I claim that an 'us' cannot be built without a 'them', I draw from a poststructuralist reflection. It's a reflection which is heavily influenced by Saussure and by the idea of the relational character of identities, which is at the core of the critique of essentialism. What I do is highlight the consequences of such reflection for the field of politics, and point out its relevance for the constitution of political identities.

I believe that once we've understood that all identities are relational and that the affirmation of a difference is the precondition for the existence of any identity, we can understand why politics (which always deals with collective identities) has to do with the constitution of an 'us' that requires as its very condition of existence the demarcation of a 'them'. Those who oppose this might say: 'Why can't we create a completely inclusive 'us'? The answer is that it's not possible, because to have an 'us' we need a 'them'. The same applies to the idea of a consensus without exclusion; to have a consensus you must have an outside to the consensus, because a consensus which doesn't have an outside is empty.

I think it's important to introduce, even if in a simplified way, these philosophical elements which are at the base of our reflection, in order to highlight the fact that all reflections take place within a philosophical perspective. Any attempt to think about the political has to be based on ontological presuppositions which cannot be proven. Evidently other people might not accept those philosophical premises because, as Derrida pointed out, any form of theoretical reflection is based on 'ethical-theoretical' decisions that serve as its point of departure, and those departure points can never have an ultimate foundation. It's not about proving 'the truth' of the conception one is defending, but about demonstrating how it allows us to understand many phenomena that other conceptions cannot apprehend. That's why, in a way, my justifications are always of a pragmatic nature. I don't claim to know the truth, because I don't think 'the truth' exists in such matters. But I can argue for my conception in a pragmatic way – showing, for instance, how from the premise that identities are always class-based, there are many phenomena which can't be understood, while a discursive perspective allows you to understand them. That's why, for instance, liberalism has always been incapable of understanding a phenomenon like nationalism, as it has to do with collective subjects.

This takes us the question of the passions, which we haven't discussed yet. In all my books, I have insisted on the importance of the passions for politics, because I think in the creation of an 'us' there is a crucial element which is connected to the affective dimension. By 'passions' I mean 'common affects', the kind of affects that are mobilised in the political arena in the constitution of us/them forms of identification. We tend to talk about 'identities' but in reality they are always 'identifications', since, according to the anti-essentialist perspective, identity is never given and therefore always a form of identification. I think psychoanalysis is key to addressing these forms of identification. To Freud, the social bond is of libidinal nature, and he highlights the crucial role played by libidinal affective bonds in collective identification processes. As he pointed out in *Group Psychology and the Analysis of the Ego*, the group is kept together by virtue of the power of Eros. Thus, acknowledging that affects provide the foundations for an 'us' is key to understanding the crucial role they play both in the establishment of a hegemony and in the counter-hegemonic struggle.

Sometimes people ask me why I talk about 'passions' rather than emotions. It's because 'emotions' doesn't seem adequate for my type of reflection as my work is in the political arena, which, as I've repeatedly highlighted, is a sphere characterised by collective identities. That's something which the term 'emotions' doesn't evoke, since emotions are generally conceived of in individual terms.

Undoubtedly, 'passions' can also be of individual nature but I prefer to use that term – with its slightly more violent connotations – because it allows me to emphasise the dimension of conflict, and to suggest a confrontation between collective political identities, something which I consider to be constitutive of politics. In the case of Podemos it seems you are fully aware of the affective dimension of politics?

ÍE: Yes we are. The slogan of the initial campaign for the European elections in May 2014 was: 'When was the last time you were excited about voting? – something no traditional party could have afforded to say. Affective involvement as an engine of mobilisation has been key to us: the recovery of the joy of being together, the solidarity between strangers – so present in our rallies and events – the belief in victory and its fearless affirmation. From the very first day we said 'we're here to win, we've had enough of resignation and complaints'. And finally, a certain spirit of 'plebeian vengeance' – non-violent – has emerged from the perception that those at the top have for too long been taking us for fools, and that now, as they experience the first tiny tremor, they are showing clear signs of unease. This democratic levelling energy is an indispensable ingredient of all progressive and emancipatory changes.

At a theoretical level, as you say, it's necessary to confront the idea that in politics, emotions or passions are the opposite of reason – that the immature societies of the South have passion in their politics, while in the mature societies of the North, rational individuals decide their vote after dispassionately reading the brochure and the elements of each political option: 'that one suits me better than the other'. In reality, there has never been any research demonstrating that things work that way. The affective dimension of politics has nothing to do with people being more or less clever; what is evident, rather, is that our choice of stance, of collective loyalties, always includes the feeling of solidarity that is created when people who do not know each other personally feel part of the same thing. Such feelings, if denied, escape politics to go elsewhere. For instance, in the phenomenon of football teams: the passion present in those contexts, even among people who don't particularly like football, is the friend-foe passion, feeling part of the same collective. The excitement in a football match comes from the eagerness to defeat the opponents, from striving for victory. The match might end in a draw, but that results from being unable to win, not from a friendly National Agreement.

CM: Well, as for that friend-enemy passion you talk about, I would prefer to refer to its agonistic form of battle between adversaries.

ÍE: Well, it's friend-enemy because supporters occasionally kill each other. It's undesirable, but violence constitutes the ultimate possibility, it is part of the clash.

CM: They may kill each other, yes, but luckily it's not usual. And one tries to avoid it.

ÍE: But that's where the intensity comes from. Passion comes from the intensity of the clash. I feel part of the same thing, of an 'us', along with many people who chant like me.

CM: But Íñigo, in agonistic battles there is also passion between the adversaries.

ÍE: Yes, but I think that passion always entails the possibility of antagonism. Agonism among opponents is an antagonism between enemies that has been institutionalised.

CM: True, but the goal is for that confrontation to be an agonistic one between adversaries, rather than a friend/enemy antagonistic one. I'd like to insist on the fact that agonism does not eliminate antagonism; it sublimates it. Clearly, there is always the possibility of antagonism suddenly resurging. Precisely because agonism doesn't cancel out antagonism, there can be no guarantee.

ÍE: In our case, the March for Change on 31 January in Madrid was a quantum leap in the sort of affections and subjectivity being created. It was no longer about people saying 'No' to things, rejecting antipopular and damaging measures against people's interests; it was fundamentally about people saying 'Yes'. Saying 'Yes' with a kind of hope, of affection, that comes from that shared passion of feeling that together we can make a difference. That seems to set in motion a collective energy which is always at the heart of all movements of democratic political change. That plebeian energy, of common people saying: 'this time it might be me, this time we might win'.

7. Consensus at the centre and right-wing populism

CM: Feeling that your vote could actually contribute to bringing about change is crucial. Believing that your vote will make a real difference – this is fundamental. This is interesting because the current post-political model of 'consensus at the centre' removes from politics one of its constitutive elements – its partisan nature. As we have seen, in order to belong to an 'us' there needs to be a 'them', and what 'them' means in the field of democratic politics is an adversary. I think that in many countries one of the reasons that fewer and fewer people are interested in politics, and there are increasing levels of abstention, is that the difference between centre-right and centre-left is so miniscule that people feel that there is actually nothing at stake. Let me remind you of a staggering electoral episode. In the very first round of the 2002 French presidential elections, Jean-Marie Le Pen eliminated the Socialist candidate, Lionel Jospin. I used to joke with my students that the difference between Jospin and Chirac was the same as that between Coca-Cola and Pepsi. Jospin – who, incidentally, is a very decent person – had the very bad idea of proclaiming during the campaign against Chirac: 'I am not a socialist'. Thereafter, most of my friends told me that they would not vote for Jospin in the first round, only in the second. People did not get mobilised for Jospin because there was no passion involved. And so Le Pen got through to the second round, leaving the Socialists out in the cold.

ÍE: This is because nothing of any substance was in dispute. The most important decisions are taken by unelected powers in a remote sphere that is far removed from any potential control by citizens. Meanwhile political representatives come to resemble each other more and more, and their constituents less and less. In the absence of any contestation over ideas and projects, democracy languishes and resignation spreads; and disaffection also breeds, as the crisis of representation deepens and institutions are increasingly under the sway of powerful minorities.

CM: That is precisely what is needed in politics: something substantial has to be at stake, with citizens having a choice between clearly different projects.

ÍE: In my opinion, with this 'post-political' narrowing of democracy, the majority of decisions – and the most crucial ones – are being taken in places that are out of the reach of popular sovereignty. And what is then left for popular sovereignty is merely to choose between variations on the same consensus, not to decide between alternatives. That cannot make a real difference to the lives of citizens! And it is certainly unlikely to galvanise any kind of passion. It is unsurprising, in these circumstances, that people abandon politics to the 'experts' or leave it at the mercy of the intricate machineries.

CM: I agree. This is why in many countries people are not interested in politics. And the development of right-wing populism is one of the consequences of this. It has to be acknowledged that right-wing populists, as is currently the case with Marine Le Pen in France, often have a much better grasp of the nature of the political struggle than progressives. For instance, they understand the formation of collective identities, and recognise that politics consists in building an 'us'. Right-wing populists also understand the role of common affects – what I call the passions – in the construction of an 'us', as well as the importance of symbols and the need to offer an alternative. Obviously, the alternative they offer is not only illusory but also completely unacceptable to progressives. But the problem is that parties on the left tend to believe that the only response is to appeal to reason. Trying to awaken passions is something that the fascist right does.

ÍE: That happens a lot in Spain, particularly among liberals who call themselves 'progressive'. They see every collective passion as carrying within itself the germ of totalitarianism. But this position means renouncing any form of collective ideal; and, when coupled with the assumption that we are in a sort of timelessness, at the end of history, it represents the abandonment of any possibility of tackling injustice. For these kinds of liberals, any attempt to mobilise passions through forms of affective identification is potentially totalitarian – for them our mature, or contemporary, freedoms are the freedoms of solitary individuals who make decisions dispassionately, and preferably not in the streets but from the comfort of their own sofas. Liberals of this kind have been horrified at our emphasis on reclaiming emotion for politics and regaining the joy of sharing collective forms of identification.

What you say about reactionary forms of populism or right-wing populism is very interesting – not only in terms of the phenomenon itself, but for what it reveals about current developments, and the possibilities that they open up in our societies, including questions about who will occupy that space if it is not occupied by democratic forces. Reactionary populism has been able to recuperate the powerful idea of 'community' – that we must build a spirit of community at a time when there is more insecurity, more anxiety and fear, more uncertainty about tomorrow. They have been able to reconstruct the idea of community as a powerful and 'efficient' idea – one that liberal-conservatives have been too quick to discard as fantasy.

CM: And it wasn't difficult for them to reclaim that ideal of community, given that the theorists of the Third Way were proclaiming that collective identities had become obsolete and that we had finally entered the era of individualism.

ÍE: Then there is the issue of politically incorrect speech. A bold anti-establishment discourse that unhesitatingly challenges the vocabularies and ways of thinking of the elite, and willingly accepts the possibility of being attacked for this, is crucial in times when traditional loyalties are breaking down. Audacity is crucial, even if it involves accepting that the adversary may hit you back all the harder. And if the democratic and progressive forces do not adopt a bold stance, we can be sure that the extreme right will do so.

For our part, Podemos was born fighting (with humility but also with determination) a certain timidity that we perceived within the existing left, which seemed to have forgotten that it takes courage to demand democracy and rights – to restore respect for the underdog – and this may well require taking sides, and losing the sympathy of the privileged, even forfeiting their pats on the back. When a measure is unjust, we must dare to name it as such and challenge it. That is what we have done, and we are paying for it. The reaction of all the usual defenders of the status quo has been fierce. Perhaps the difference between the diverse ways of building popular identities is essentially this: who is the adversary, who do you oppose?

CM: Anti-establishment discourse can be articulated in different ways, and that is why it is very important not to leave it to the forces of the right. In the case of Greece it is clear that if Syriza had not existed, the neo-Nazi party Golden Dawn would by now have been getting better results.

ÍE: Yes, and this raises the question of how to combat right-wing populism. There is a widespread but clearly mistaken notion on the left that if we also adopt a 'popular' approach we could be paving the way for their ideas. On the contrary, I think it helps them much more if we abandon all forms of collective affects, and thus cede this space to them. Another serious mistake is to relinquish to them the battle for hegemony in the sphere of national identification. It is a mistake to hand over to the most reactionary forces the opportunity to put forward, uncontested, their own view of what the country stands for – their project for a strong country will in reality be built against the weak, against outsiders, against national minorities, or simply be based on chauvinism. They will not be trying to rebuild a civic, popular and democratic idea of the country, one that is supportive and inclusive, and endowed with solid institutions and democratic safeguards – in other words a democratic, progressive and popular patriotism.

CM: I find it a real problem that the left largely has a very negative attitude towards the very idea of patriotism, as if patriotism could only manifest itself in reactionary ways.

ÍE: The struggle for hegemony, for national identification, is key. And another important point is to try to understand how the far right, which is not classist – that is to say, does not base its policy on social classes – has managed to engage with a diverse and wider array of sectors, and, potentially, to build broader national-popular blocks.

CM: They are the true Gramscians!

ÍE: Right-wing Gramscians.

CM: Yes, absolutely. Unfortunately they have understood Gramsci better than most sectors of the left. I remember when – before writing *Hegemony and Socialist Strategy* – I published my first article on Gramsci, in which I tried to defend a non-economistic reading of his concept of hegemony, and my interpretation was criticised by Marxists like Perry Anderson. It so happened that at that time we were both in Caracas, holding seminars at the CENDES in Venezuela, and we were both talking about Gramsci. The students were quite perplexed because we were proposing divergent readings. At the same time in France the 'New Right' – an intellectual group directed by Alain Benoit – was organising a symposium to promote a 'right-wing Gramscianism', insisting on the importance of the struggle for hegemony. The left, meanwhile, could not understand the nature of this struggle for hegemony, because they interpreted it in terms of the imposition of the dominant ideology. And I am concerned that

Gramsci's contribution has still not been really assimilated by the left.

8. The 15 May Movement and the emergence of Podemos

ÍE: To understand why reactionary populism has not gained much of a grip in Spain we need to look closely at the appearance here of two 'democratic vaccines': on the one hand, the role of the 15 May movement (known in Spain as 15M), and on the other the emergence of Podemos. I think that 15M served as a vaccine that prevented discontent from taking a reactionary form, and instead helped to articulate a collective demand for a broadening of rights and an expansion of democracy – for more universality of rights and more democracy, instead of more restrictions and less democracy. 15M did not change the balance of forces within the state, but it did nevertheless successfully help sow the seeds of a cultural shift.

CM: I have my reservations regarding this point. To some extent I agree with you. However, I believe that 15M would have come to nothing without Podemos, which finally managed to capitalise on all that energy. Without Podemos, might there have developed a dangerous form of scepticism and cynicism that could have shifted things in a reactionary direction? I think that could have been the case. That is the reason why it's very important to channel these protest movements in a direction that seeks to engage with existing institutions in order to transform them. The explosion of protests is a first step, but without a second moment of channelling a movement can acquire a direction other than progressive.

ÍE: Yes, absolutely. Here there are several issues worth commenting on. 15M could be seen as a sort of horizontal expansion of discontent. On the one hand, many people were driven to gather together by a radical opposition to the status quo, but, on the other, this position helped to *politicise* certain issues that were previously seen as private grievances. If you've had to leave your country to find work, or you're stuck at home with your parents, or have to hold down several jobs to make ends meet, or you feel that the privileged elite will always have the upper hand and be in government no matter how you vote ... these are not private problems, they are immediately inscribed in the public sphere.

There was a very significant moment in the protests in Puerta del Sol when many people affixed post-it notes written in the first person, notes telling about their particular individual situation.[7] That was an initial moment that Gramsci would call 'economic-corporate'. It was people saying: I have this or that problem. But the sharing of these problems helped establish them as problems of the public agenda: they could no longer be ignored. This democratised the public agenda and prevented the usual split between the official-institutional agenda and the concerns of ordinary people with less ability to influence the institutions. And this in turn put the elites on the defensive. The elites aged quickly after 15M; and although they continued to govern, 15M had an overriding impact on the common sense of the time. It

---

7 Puerta del Sol is one of the main squares in Madrid, and is where the Indignados/15M camped out in 2011.

did not transform anything, it did not constitute political actors capable of leading a war of position within the state, but it definitely created a climate, a state of perceptions, that opened the possibility for political change. So whenever we are questioned about the relationship between Podemos and 15M – and abroad we are constantly asked this question – we say that Podemos is not the party of 15M.

CM: I think it is important that you clarify this issue because for many people the relationship between Podemos and 15M is unclear.

ÍE: We are not the party of 15M – mainly because any party that claimed to be the party of 15M would be a fraud. It is impossible to have a 'party of 15M', given that it is a heterogeneous movement, a phenomenon which expands horizontally by putting together very different grievances and discontents, some with very weak links with each other, articulated only by their common opposition to power. So 15M neither has nor can have a party – yet not because it is not desirable ...

CM: What is more, they did not want to have a relationship with political parties.

ÍE: Some of them didn't. I would say that by shouting 'they do not represent us' 15M participants wanted to express a crisis of political representation *tout-court*, but that events after 15M demonstrate that, for most of the people coming out to protest, or just to show their sympathy, this did not imply a rejection of all forms of representation. They were not saying that they did not want to be represented. They were, rather, throwing down a challenge to the elites who at present monopolise representation. It may seem a paradox, but in fact, as with many other movements that actually sow the seeds of change in history, 15M was born as a 'conservative' reaction: citizens coming out to protest against losing already acquired or promised rights, demanding that the elite is not placed above the law, and that the established framework for coexistence is respected. This is why we say that, in an exceptional time like this, as a result of the brazen offensive of the oligarchy, ideas of change are by now well anchored in common sense, because the elites have gone so far. That suggests unprecedented political possibilities.

That's why Podemos is not the expression or the electoral translation of 15M. First, because there cannot be one; and secondly because the project of Podemos was launched without any previous consultation between movements, or between assemblies, or among the indignados. It is an initiative of activists and citizens who have resolved that there is scope to convert a portion ...

CM: Of course, it would not have been possible if they had decided to discuss the initiative with all movements.

ÍE: Obviously. If we had subjected the project to discussion of that sort it would have never been born. At this point we need to remember how infrequent self-criticism is in Spain: most sections of the movement, political parties, all the forces that called themselves the left, everyone – agreed that the project made no sense at all and that it would be a failure. Some of them even put it plainly in writing. If the idea had undergone a process of assembly-based discussion, it would have never come to anything. But maybe the difference between giving your opinion and acting as a militant lies in accepting the challenge of putting your hypothesis to the test.

We are still living a paradoxical situation in which you need to do the opposite of what some sectors of activists recommend in order to secure new arrangements and to achieve broad popular recognition.

The electoral campaign conducted by Podemos consisted of doing, step by step, precisely the opposite of what would be recommended by the most militant groups. Everyone predicted that it would go totally wrong. The truth is, however, that we have experienced such a massive transformation that the old certainties that are seen as stable and unquestionable amongst the ghettos of radical militancy are now revealed for what they are: a form of consensus that removes the possibility of change, or any opportunity to make a successful challenge to majority groups and turn outrage into power. For all their diversity, these groups inhabit precisely the discursive spaces that are left to them by the establishment, and they are, essentially, satisfied with a trade-off between 'purity' and marginality.

The closer you get to that consensus, the further away you go from the possibility of a new consensus with a number of popular sectors that are clearly unhappy but nonetheless without political reference points.

All of the aforementioned allows us to say that Podemos does not spring out of 15M. It is not its political or electoral expression. In addition, a good portion of the discontent was not part of 15M, although it sympathised with it, certainly. Yet I must say, without the movement of 15M and without the small changes in common sense that followed, the window of opportunity that opened for something like Podemos to come into existence would have not occurred. In that moment when, although 70 to 80 per cent of Spaniards were sympathetic to what you would identify as the main motives or claims of 15M, the Popular Party still obtained an absolute majority in the ensuing elections.

The key to what happened is not how many people went out to protest, or how many meetings and assemblies flourished, though admittedly the numbers were very impressive, with all the logistics that were involved and the demonstrative aspect. The key is the subterranean, magmatic change, thanks to which the cultural climate changes, in a manner that means that issues that were not politicised before are today felt as increasingly intolerable, and thus presented to the rulers as such. Moreover, there is the growing perception that a political cycle is running out, and as it comes to an end another one must open. These adjustments to the common sense of the time are precisely what allow people to imagine the building of an exceptional political intervention.

That was the moment when we came to believe that a different majority was possible, a transversal one, as well as a consensus around a number of ideas that are already common sense but actually run across the Spanish political spectrum: this is the reason for the claim that Podemos cannot be described in terms of left or right.[8] It is not at all a renunciation of ideology, because, as you know, ideologies

8 Transversal is another word that is more commonly used in Spanish and Italian than English. The term gives expression to the idea of a democratic practice that looks for commonalities without asserting universalism: notions of difference are seen as encompassing, not replacing, equality. According to Cynthia Cockburn and Lynette Hunter, 'Transversal politics is the practice of creatively crossing (and redrawing) the borders that mark significant politicised differences'.

are expressed – and have been expressed in most of the planet for most of history – in different metaphors, on the left and right alike. And it is not a marketing operation that window-dresses the essence of things with different clothes to get the vote, not at all; the crux of the matter is that the frontier drawn by the new democratic majority cannot be described with the usual left-right wording. This wording has fuelled the Spanish political regime for the last thirty years whilst keeping safe the interests of the privileged at the expense of the majority of the people.

CM: This is an issue that we will have to discuss later on. Now, going back to a previous question: what is the misperception on the part of all these political activists that explains their failure to understand the importance of the institutional dimension? In the case of liberalism, as we discussed before, they do not recognise the importance of collective movements; neither do they recognise antagonism. Clearly, there is no surprise here: they cannot understand politics. But in the case of activists in these movements, what is preventing them from making a proper analysis of the situation?

ÍE: For a certain sector identified with the theories of the *multitude,* a minority that was nevertheless intellectually influential, 15M was the beginning of a victory. A victory that would perhaps take some time. They kept on saying that institutions were just zombies, that they were no more than the walking dead. But some of us replied: 'For zombies they are surprisingly lively, privatising and evicting like mad …'.

Let us say that theirs was an overly optimistic view: 'we are winning'. Besides, this view was indebted to a very *Zapatista* vision, or *neo-Zapatista*, according to which 'we go slowly because the road is long'; or, for instance, 'we are making changes at the micro level, molecular changes that are perhaps not as visible as the institutional changes you propose but are the true passport to a new world'; in this view also, 'this is a slower process, transforming everyday life' ... in summary, everything under this approach is always an apology for the *micro* and an apology for *procedure*. Thus, for them we are already winning, given that any attempt to transform this potentiality into an effective political impact on the state would give the state the ability to recapture it or to integrate it; and that would be a mistake because it would decapitate the 'truly democratic potentiality' of the movement.

Let me clarify my position. Many of the activists who subscribe to the views I have just described have undoubtedly invested a lot of energy and creativity into their movement, but from my point of view their perception of things is mistaken.

It seems to me that they are replacing the w*hy* with the *how*: because we are not always sure what the target is, we have discussions about procedures, and evade some of the difficult questions, such as the construction of a will to power or the question of the state.

CM: That is the view of the protest movements and, as you see, the problem of part of the radical left.

ÍE: For much of the more traditional left, 15M is an expression of downright naivety; and for the most mistaken among them, it is something even worse, perhaps having been nurtured within the murky corridors of power. According to this section of the left, nothing changes after 15M; it does not represent a cultural shift and is a profound mistake, because it is nowhere to be found in the handbook: the protesters are not dressed in blue overalls, they do not carry hammers and so on and so forth; in summary, for these sectors of the traditional left 15M is useless.

Then there is another perspective, a religious and aesthetic position that, although it is not very sophisticated in theoretical terms, I think is right. Put briefly, it says that daring to win involves getting your hands dirty, assuming contradictions and accepting small victories, because in the struggle you win some and negotiate the rest, this is to say, you push forward and you get stained. You have to roll up your sleeves and swallow the messy reality, and this is definitely less comfortable than the 'purity' of defeat.

Moreover, some of the radical sectors seem to be enamoured with defeat. This romantic infatuation explains, for example, why a Latin American president who transforms the lives of his people is less attractive than, let us say, Salvador Allende, who was killed in the Palacio de la Moneda; and I say this with the utmost respect for Allende and the experience of Popular Unity in Chile. But on this view a slain hero is greater hero ... a slain hero is fantastic because he hasn't had the opportunity to get contaminated by reality. Pure as an angel he dies, with his horn-rimmed glasses and European look, a doctor ... and he becomes an icon. That kind of infatuation is a form of maximalism, a refusal to take a gamble and dare to win, with all the unavoidable complications that entails.

Then there is the question, as we noted above, of the state. If you understand the state as a machine rather than a field of forces (a machine that can be besieged, or destroyed, or from which you can escape), it can only be accepted or rejected as a whole. This prevents an understanding of the state as a terrain for struggle, a place within which there is a balance of forces – an always unstable balance, an ever-moving 'equilibrium'; it is fortified by existing institutions, but is also a battlefield in a struggle that, especially when the weather is stormy for the establishment, always remains unresolved.

CM: I agree with you. The question of the state is fundamental. On the one side are those who see it as a neutral institution that requires no modification. On the other there are those who see it as a pure form of domination that needs to be destroyed. Yet few people actually realise that the state is a site of contestation with which we must engage deeply in order to transform it at the service of the popular forces. This lack of understanding of the nature of the state is the origin of many of the mistakes of the left in its various forms.

ÍE: The refusal to understand the state also implies a refusal to understand questions of representation and leadership. For such a stance or theory these are just one-way phenomena; representation is not for them a negotiation between the represented and their representatives, but instead an almost 'magical' transfer.

From the same standpoint, leadership is not a relationship of 'listening-proposing-listening', that is to say, a relationship in which, in order to represent interests, you must also interpret what is emerging from below. No. For leaders of that type, 'below' does not exist, and 'leadership' is just an impersonation of sovereignty. We have to acknowledge that we come from a tradition of thirty years of cultural and intellectual defeat for the left. The theoretical and intellectual ingredients that we draw on in our discussions were, and still are, very weak. We don't have many reference points for our thinking, or much practical experience that could rejuvenate theory and debate. For several decades we haven't experienced a time like these 'weeks of real movement' that have taught us more than ten treatises put together ...

9. Latin America and experiences of the national-popular

CM: What led you to think differently?

ÍE: In my case, what was decisive for my political thinking was exposure to the popular constituent processes of political transformation and state reform in Latin America. It's impossible to find out anything about these processes from Spain, where all you hear about in the media is a continuous and terrifying disaster, a process that infantilises its societies so that they keep electing the same people. For some of us, it's been a great help to experience these processes that have been capable of translating discontent into a collective, national-popular will that can have an impact on the state. This politics cannot do everything, but it brings about processes of state reform and transition.

But saying that these developments help us to think and test categories, doesn't mean they are simply models to imitate. They are not reference points for our situation, because of obvious major cultural, geopolitical, and economic differences. Our societies in the west are not broken, and they have not experienced the brutal levels of impoverishment seen in Latin America at the turn of the twentieth century. In our case, progressive political practices don't have to face the challenge of building a national state practically from scratch.

In Latin America, some of the popular forces have undertaken historical tasks – civic inclusion, the creation of public services, fiscal reform – similar to those social democracy developed in Europe, though with more turbulence, because of oligarchic resistance and the lack of a periphery that could bear the costs. Political change in Spain and southern Europe is necessary precisely to prevent a drift – through a vicious spiral of debt-cuts-poverty – towards the kind of social fragmentation and institutional collapse that characterised the lost decade of the 1990s in a number of Latin American countries. But here, it's not a question of bringing anything down, but of preventing the selfishness and incapacity of those in power from destroying the institutions and protective mechanisms that are our societies' collective heritage.

CM: Yes, you said previously that for you the decisive factor was your experience in Latin America, which led you to see things differently. That was in a way your 'road to Damascus'.

ÍE: Yes, I've been involved in activism since I was 14, and for a long time I had a very different approach and conception of politics. For some time, I was heavily influenced by Italian theorists of autonomy, and by some of the practices of Italian intellectuals, who fascinated us in their radicalism and theoretical sophistication. Later, I started combining that scaffolding with different authors in a disorderly manner – with some Gramsci from early on. But then I landed in Latin America, and I soon realised that the categories I had brought with me were insufficient; they didn't help me to understand what was happening around me. Not because there was some sort of different cultural essence or through the experience of a post-colonial 'new age', but because I encountered phenomena that made me think about the national, the state, power, hegemony, though I was coming largely from a politics of resistance.

CM: In a way something similar happened to me. I was a fairly orthodox Althusserian, and it was the years I spent in Colombia teaching philosophy in Bogotá's National University that made me change my perspective. That's why I decided to come back to Europe to specialise in political science, and to start working on Gramsci.

ÍE: For my part, when I arrived in Bolivia in 2006 I was heavily influenced by my experiences in the anti-globalisation movement, during which a great deal of my first political socialisation took place, and by the European reception of Zapatism; and I had also been influenced by the waves of protests in Argentina on 19 and 20 December 2001, the Brazilian Landless Rural Workers' Movement, and the water and gas war in Bolivia – but not by the subsequent electoral process, which was of less interest to me at that time.

Soon after arriving in Bolivia I discovered the idea of the national-popular, not yet as a theoretical construction, but as something I experienced, touched and read. Not through those who theorised about it, but through those who developed it, the theorists of the national popular experiences across the continent. I was already interested in the phenomenon of national construction, starting with the Catalan case, but in Latin America, with popular nationalism, I discovered a whole new dimension.

I encountered the national-popular phenomenon, which I found fascinating, both in its ambivalence and in the vigour of its political identifications, which, while far from loose, didn't articulate on the left/right axis. I was interested in the popular and its construction.

I also started to think about the state as an object of study and serious activism, because I lived through, worked and advised on, and was present at, the processes though which plebeian or subaltern coalitions were gaining access to the state, coalitions that had entered into a part of the state, the government, but were surrounded by conservative powers intent on limiting the scope of the changes. I thus lived through a war of position inside the state, which I witnessed from within. I experienced the difficulties of trying out new ideas, but, far from this being discouraging, it opened up a whole new field of research which I found fascinating. I also learned to appreciate how much effort conquests take, and how to build in irreversibility, which from then on would become a central object of intellectual preoccupation for me. I remember discovering a statistic in Bolivia that showed that, since the beginning of the process of political change, and as a result of a better access to milk, children now weighed more. And I remember thinking that perhaps this wasn't quite socialism, but that only a fool would dismiss an achievement like that, after all the effort it had taken to consolidate this precarious popular advance.

Thinking back on it now, I find it surprising that nobody has yet undertaken a critical analysis of the events, actors and strategies embraced during the crisis of the neoliberal model in Latin America. The Zapatistas, the MST, the *que se vayan todos* [out with them all] and picketing assemblies, and all the theoretical constructions that saw in these protests a matrix of practices that were capable of changing their countries in favour of the many, building counterpowers outside the state: 'changing the world without taking power'.[9]

Seen from today's perspective, the outcome is heart-breaking: where there wasn't an electoral victory and access to the state, so as to be able to wage a war of position between emancipatory and conservative or oligarchic forces from the inside, there was regression as soon as social mobilisations died down – and they always die down. As a result, today the living standards of ordinary people are much worse.

CM: For some on the left in Europe, the influence of the experiences of Latin America has taken a very different form from the one you and I have taken. It seems strange to me, for instance, to see how certain sections of the European left still present the experience of the 'piqueteros' in Argentina as a model to follow. In the literature promoting the exodus strategy, it is common to find a celebration of this movement of the unemployed which, towards the end of the 1990s, started organising street blockades to protest against the neoliberal policies of President Carlos Menem – and these were, incidentally, the groups which also organised in cooperatives during the 2001-02 economic crisis, and were very active in the popular protests that brought down Fernando de la Rua's government. With their *que se vayan todos* slogan they proclaimed their rejection of all politicians and called for a self-organisation of popular sectors. The exodus theorists see in these piqueteros a paradigmatic example of the political expression of the multitude, and present their refusal to collaborate with political

9 *Que se vayan todos* was the main slogan of the protests of December 2001 in Argentina.

parties as a model for the desertion strategy. They don't seem to realise that what the piquetero movement shows is precisely the limits of that strategy. They undoubtedly contributed to the overthrow of a president, but when the time came to offer an alternative, their refusal to participate in elections made them incapable of influencing the course of events that followed. If it wasn't for the fact that Néstor Kirchner won the elections and started to implement progressive measures to restore the Argentinian economy and improve the situation of the poor, the result of the popular protests would have been very different. The democratic advances in Argentina under the governments of Néstor Kirchner and Cristina Fernández de Kirchner took place thanks to the synergies established between the government and a series of social movements with the goal of tackling the social and socioeconomic challenges faced by the country. Far from offering a successful example of the desertion strategy, the Argentinian case reveals the limitations of such a strategy. It highlights the importance of combining parliamentary and extra-parliamentary struggles in a common battle to transform the power configurations within the framework of pluralist democracy.

ÍE: That experience is important. Many of the people who ran for election did not come from an already constituted force; in other words, they didn't win because they already had strength, but because they participated in an electoral process that articulated a new identity – so much so that Kirchnerism is now a defined and relatively new political space in Argentina, still with capacity for power. However, to fully assess the impact of Kirchnerism it would be necessary to undertake an evaluation of the living standards of the population today.

In many Latin American countries, neoliberal reforms and

the impoverishment they brought found themselves up against deep political crises and waves of social contestation, some strong enough to veto those reforms. In some of them, electoral contests became plebiscites between the decaying order and a new incipient popular will, which opened the door to the formation of governments able to launch constituent or state reform processes, and to develop transformative public policies that have improved the lives of those at the bottom of society.

In the places where social contestation didn't have an impact on the state, and social movements gave up the dispute for power, the advances achieved by social mobilisations were overturned as soon as the mobilisations died down, or the situation of exceptionality 'calmed down'. Conversely, in places where the discontent produced a plebeian irruption into the state – with all the more or less unavoidable contradictions and problems that brings – the launch of transition processes created a virtuous cycle that has taken millions of people out of poverty while at the same time building national and regional sovereignty. I think it's obvious to what experiences I'm referring to here. It would be useful to undertake a critical analysis of them, as some of them were very beautiful, and very well-regarded by the European left, but haven't actually changed their countries and eventually ended in impasse. I'm not saying that it always has to be like that, or that those examples express a paradigm. I'm simply talking about what happened during that specific period in Latin America.

My final point here is that in our societies one kind of political power is derived from the ability to convince and to express that conviction, including in electoral battles; but the other kind comes, as Mao Zedong said, 'from the barrel of the gun' – from the capacity for coercion. These are of course two ideal types, this is a simplification. But these are the two extremes that mark the options in decisive situations, which can settle the question of power. There are not that many other options; in other words, there are no other paradigms of access to, or construction of, political power.

CM: I find it really worrying that in the vast majority of countries in South America, many of the so-called 'left' are against the national-popular governments. In Argentina, the self-proclaimed left is against Kirchnerism, in Ecuador it's against Correa's government.

ÍE: Yes, but that's because these national-popular governments have also broken the rules of the traditional political game, and the symbolic geographies of parliamentary politics. All the popular experiences in Latin America have been heretical, and as part of this heresy they have broken the rules of identification. They have built a national identification of a plebeian and popular nature, which has displaced and confused both liberal and conservative sectors, as well as a substantial part of the cosmopolitan or Eurocentric left, which I think has traditionally misunderstood the situation in their own countries.

All the great moments of advance for the masses have gone against the grain of history – and against the rules of the bibles of revolution. They've always had their own logic, their own national traits, and defied the rules with regard to – among other things – tactical decisions, modes of articulation, demands for nodal points, and bonds between different social sectors.

Naturally, all the manuals have been written in Europe – and if they have never worked here, how would you expect them to work there? The appeal of the Peruvian writer José Carlos Mariategui comes to mind – for a socialism that was 'neither a replica nor a copy' of the European models. One that is capable of taking into account, for instance, the comprehension of, and appeal to, 'the indigenous', beyond the narrowness of classist models. Ultimately, it's a question of asserting the importance of the particularities of each cultural context and each political setting.

I think all the national-popular experiences have made many people nervous: populist-type constructions have displaced and confused both a great number of conservative groups, and a substantial part of the left, not only in Latin America but also in closer latitudes.

This is a shame because it deprives emancipatory thought of an applied field of discussion, around which it could eluci-date or test questions and options. It is as if those experiences – together with their difficulties, successes, and mistakes – don't deserve to be rigorously studied and discussed. And this represents a failure to give due recognition to a region that is currently, objectively-speaking, a progressive and democratic pole in global geopolitics.

CM: The element that you identify as 'heretical' in those expe-riences is without doubt one of the reasons for the current hostility to the progressive governments in South America among part of the left in Europe. In France, for instance, *Libération* is terribly critical, as are others like *Le Monde*, and in other countries *The Guardian* or *El País*. I don't know a single so-called progressive newspaper in Europe that presents what happens in South America in an even minimally objective way. And if you ask these people on the left why they reject these experiences, they say it's because that is not the left, that is populism. They contrast a 'good left' with a 'bad left'. The good one would be that of Michelle Bachelet's Chilean socialism, which is of course the closest to the European model, and the bad one would be that of Venezuela, with Brazil and Argentina about half way between the two. It's interesting to see how the Bolivian model, which initially generated a lot of sympathy due to its indigenous character, its 'exotic' nature, has now become part of the 'bad left', after Evo Morales got closer to Hugo Chávez.

In trying to find an explanation for this attitude, I reached the conclusion that it has to do with the way pluralist democracy is understood here, and with the attempt to impose a specific interpretation – that which is currently hegemonic in Europe – as the only legitimate one. This shows the European left cannot accept the legitimacy of democratic institutions different from those found in Europe. In *The Democratic Paradox*, which studies the nature of the Western model of democracy, pluralist democracy, I describe it as consisting of the articulation of two different traditions: the tradition of political liberalism, with its idea of the rule of law, of individual freedom and human rights; and the democratic tradition of equality and popular sovereignty.

Unlike those who claim there is a necessary union between those two traditions, I agree with the Canadian philosopher C.B. Macpherson that it is a contingent historical articulation, established in the nineteenth century as a result of the joint participation of liberals and democrats in struggles against absolutism. Through that articulation, liberalism was democratised and democracy was liberalised. That's why the ethical-political principles of pluralist liberal democracy are freedom and equality for all.

That is, however, a contingent articulation rather than a necessary co-originality as Habermas claims. Carl Schmitt is right when he says these two logics are ultimately incompatible, as perfect freedom and perfect equality can never coexist. Schmitt claims there is therefore a contradiction between liberal and democratic principles, and that's why he considers liberal democracy an unviable regime. I, on the other hand, maintain that we need to see that impossibility of reconciliation as a tension rather than as a contradiction – a productive tension that creates the necessary space for pluralism. I think it's very important for that tension to stay alive, being constantly negotiated and renegotiated, to make sure that no element becomes ever entirely dominant – which is precisely what happened with the hegemony of neoliberalism.

ÍE: Absolutely, that's right. I've also often wondered where that hostility from European progressives to the so-called populist experiences in Latin America came from.

CM: Nowadays, in our post-democratic societies, anything connected with democracy understood as equality and popular sovereignty has been dismissed by the neoliberal hegemony. Any dimension of popular sovereignty is seen as something archaic. This has now become a fundamental part of the common sense of the European left, which has come to accept that democracy is just about elections, multi-party systems, and the recognition of human rights.

What happened in South America – which I think is relevant to the experiences of progressive governments in Europe as well – is that they recalibrated the relation between freedom and equality, putting popular sovereignty and equality back in the driving seat, but without eliminating the liberal dimension. That is why the European left, which thinks its post-democratic model is the only legitimate one, on seeing the Latin

American models says: 'that's not democracy, that's populism'. Why populism? Because they've reinvigorated the democratic element?

ÍE: I think in Latin America that contingent conjunction of liberalism and democracy never happened, or did so to a lesser extent ...

CM: That's true. They've often had liberal governments which were not democratic or democratic governments which were not liberal, as was the case in Argentina.

ÍE: This convergence happened to a lesser extent in Latin America than in Europe. As a result, some liberal principles are now being used by the traditional elites as a defence against the advance of popular sovereignty – institutions used as defensive trenches against the masses. For them it's as if any institution, simply on account of being one – even when it doesn't respond to people's needs or isn't very democratic – is preferable to the constituent irruption of the people. Or even worse, as if it is impossible for a regime to be both popular and republican – in the sense of fostering vigorous institutions, equilibrium, and the accountability of power, in a pluralist sphere. That is arguably the challenge facing the most advanced state reform processes.

This situation cannot be apprehended from within the framework of a liberal paradigm that, after decades of cynicism, now believes that individual freedoms are being threatened, not by the oligarchical powers of a minority, but by the construction of new majorities and the return of passion and big ideas to politics. To this prejudiced way of thinking, any collective ideal is always suspected of totalitarianism, and cynicism is presented as the only vaccine for it. But in reality, it is the privileged minority who are in the habit of excluding the people from their concept of democracy and putting the imprint of oligarchy onto our democratic-liberal political systems.

That fear of the popular – especially when it's outside a known frame or in its wildest or most ambivalent forms – is clearly rooted in Europe. This might be due to our history of fascist experiences, leading many to think that fascism represents the totality of populist phenomena – or, worse, that they are their ultimate hidden truth. Thus, any identification of homeland and people crystallised into an affective identification in which leadership plays a role, and involving a tense relationship with opposing forces or existing institutions, is seen as necessarily carrying within its entrails a reactionary danger. This view persists even though in other latitudes populist movements have had the opposite political character, and been based on democratisation and wealth redistribution. This not only blocks any possibility of thinking about change beyond the model of alternation within the pregiven institutions – and thus beyond a frozen balance of power; it also forgets the substantial part of European, and most certainly Latin American, history, in which the experience of the masses being included into the state were of national-popular nature.

CM: Without a doubt.

ÍE: I think this view also has a touch of epistemological colonialism: 'those are malformations because pure phenomena take place here'. An intellectually and politically aged Europe looks down on, with contempt even, these new experiences of collective will construction and transformation. Of course these experiences are always contradictory, and include many problems and mistakes – like any real experience – but they are often analysed and belittled by Europeans from a position of cynical and colonial arrogance.

CM: This is also closely related to the influence of the hegemony of neoliberalism and the common sense that has been created as a result – a common sense which conceives democracy in a strictly liberal sense, which tries to disqualify any attempt to question this situation by accusing it of 'populism'.

10. Understanding populism and 'populist situations'

ÍE: We reach here another key point of our discussion: the issue of populism and the difficulties in understanding the Latin American national-popular experiences, even among progressive sectors in Europe. Interestingly enough, this is a discussion – a set of terms and a type of debate – that has returned to Europe over the last few years. I think their initial return was because of the rise of reactionary populism, the extreme-right populism that has showed us that if 'the people' isn't constructed by the left, it will be constructed against the left.

These notions have now also returned, at least in southern Europe, as a result of what I've been analysing – in somehow provocative terms – as a 'Latin-Americanisation' of the political landscape in these countries. By this I mean a situation of progressive divorce between representatives and represented, collapse in the capacity of existing institutional models to meet citizens' demands, and increasing middle-class impoverishment. The result has been an accumulation of discontent, and a transfer of sovereignty that has made national elites look like the colonial intermediaries of unelected powers. All of this has generated a situation that has been characterised by a degree of political Latin-Americanisation, which, despite the many differences from the original in terms of economics, culture and state form, has brought 'the people' to the fore of political discussion. In Spain it's very noticeable that, since our first impact on the political arena, we've been accused of being 'populist'. In Greece, Syriza has been accused of something similar. So has Mélenchon in France, as well as an increasing number of other new actors questioning the order of the elites. What's behind that accusation, that vulgar use of the term as something vague but pejorative, a term that reviles your opponent? Why is it so commonly used by the powerful and their allied sectors in the intelligentsia and the media? The term is clearly in widespread circulation, so I think it's worth taking some time to clarify it, and to ask ourselves whether we're in fact currently living a populist situation, and if so why.

CM: I think the best way to examine the nature of populism is through Ernesto Laclau's analysis in *On Populist Reason*, where he develops a formal concept of populism. He argues that populism is a way of constructing the political; that it isn't linked to a specific ideological content or the practices of a particular group. It's just a mode of demand articulation that can take a wide range of different forms. It is a mode of articulation that operates following a logic of equivalence that results in the creation of 'a people', through a chain of equivalence linking a multiplicity of heterogeneous demands.

Laclau notes that for popular identities to exist, it is necessary to establish an internal frontier that expresses the division of the social. I don't want to go into more detail here, as it's a highly sophisticated and complex theory, but I think with this we already have a starting point for approaching the topic of populism in an analytical way that allows us to escape the shallow perspective from which it is generally approached.

ÍE: I agree with both the approach and the definition. But before we discuss it further, I would like to briefly reflect on the reasons behind the use of the term 'populism' by the elite, who can never define it other than as a denigrating weapon against their opponents. Its dominant use, both intellectual and in the media, associates it with demagogy, a resource used by political entrepreneurs to appeal to the lower passions of the poorly educated, who are willing to vote irresponsibly in times of desperation or frustration. Underlying this use is, I think, an aristocratic prejudice which would ultimately take us back to a form of census suffrage linked to the old conservative fear of the tumultuous character of the plebs in politics, and its supposed animal or infantile, and easily manipulated, instincts, especially in southern countries. Additionally – and here lies the key – this is a phenomenon that doesn't appear to affect elites or rational individuals: it's only the masses who have these demagogically excitable lower passions. And something else that underlies this old conservative utopia is the notion of a democracy without people, without collective will or conflict; as merely the dispassionate and technical management of things that have already been decided; as limited to a competition between dignitaries for audiences and electorates. This illusion – which you call post-politics – has its highest expression in a religious faith in economics as a 'science' capable of deciding what's best for a society, regardless of that society's opinion.

CM: It is very convenient for the parties of the centrist consensus to use the term populist to disqualify their opponents. The 'populism' accusation is particularly useful for the so-called 'left-wing' parties, as it allows them to avoid self-criticism, and any recognition that, having abandoned the defence of the popular classes, they are to a large extent responsible for the crisis of representation that is the underlying cause of the emergence of a wide range of 'anti-establishment' parties. They thus limit themselves to a moralising critique instead of undertaking a political analysis.

ÍE: In a recent article in the *New Left Review*, 'Populism and the New Oligarchy', Marco d'Eramo argues that we're living in a situation characterised by a paradox: the greater the disappearance of the people, the more common the negative use of the term populism becomes. The more absent 'the people' is from the dominant discourse – as a gathering of the unentitled, an entity that goes beyond the mere aggregation of individuals, voters, or consumers – and the more popular sovereignty is squeezed by the powers of privileged minorities, the more frequent become the elite's accusations of populism towards any actors or movements questioning the established order, or maintaining that things could be different, or that there's nothing natural about the growth of inequality.

CM: I think the populism accusation reveals something important about the kind of politics that is promoted by those who use the term to dismiss the parties that question the status quo. It reveals their inability to understand the political in its antagonist dimension, and the dynamics of democratic politics.

ÍE: When we organised the Podemos Conference at the Palacio Vistalegre in Madrid, in autumn 2014, we were widely commended for it, as it was seen as the right thing to do for a responsible party – it fitted the conventional institutional way of doing politics. A few months later, however, we decided to call people – citizens from across Spain – onto the streets, to the Puerta del Sol for 'the March of Change'.

This mobilisation marked a qualitative leap, as its aim was not to protest, but to affirm the construction of a popular identity around a will for political change – something that had become possible in the fast-paced 2015 electoral cycle. The march was a success, both politically and attendance-wise, but it attracted criticism and incomprehension from traditional political and media voices. Why were we doing that? Some even questioned our democratic nature, comparing the March of Change with Mussolini's March on Rome. Again we saw a quasi-aesthetic rejection, a mistrust of the masses and their passions in politics – which had also been a central feature of the Puerta del Sol on 31 January.

CM: That incomprehension doesn't surprise me. It's a consequence of their inability to understand the process of political identity formation, and the role that passions play in the creation of us/them-type identifications.

ÍE: Going back to your definition of populism, I completely agree. I've been working for some time now from Ernesto Laclau's approach, understanding populism more as form than as a content: an identity construction praxis which can then take very different ideological directions.

To understand this position it is necessary to accept a premise: that in politics, loyalties, and the positions on the board, are not fixed or predetermined by any social condition. On the contrary, they are discursively constructed through friend/foe type groupings, and are permanently subject to negotiation. This being so, a populist discourse is that which is capable of unifying very diverse positions and social sectors through a dichotomisation of the political arena based on the opposition of the traditional elites and 'the people' – or some other name designating the same kind of opposition: citizens, country, and so on. It's a construction that allows subaltern sectors to successfully demand the representation of a forgotten or betrayed general interest. It's important, however, to bear in mind that these are names and concepts, not statistical data. That is, they are symbolic constructions. They are not lies, they are real, in the sense that they group positions and generate new balances of power and new institutions. The populist moment thus obscures internal differences through its articulation of a people – differences which re-emerge later, when, following the rupture, it is time for the institutionalisation of the new equilibriums and agreements,

CM: Following Laclau's conception of populism as an equivalential articulation of heterogeneous demands, we must try to understand why we're seeing the emergence of parties with populist characteristics in so many European countries. As I've already pointed out, I think the key to this is the multiplication of demands that cannot find an expression through the traditional political channels. I think this is taking place for two reasons.

The first one has to do with the centrist consensus we've already discussed. In many European countries, this consensus has led to the implementation of a type of democracy that eliminates anything to do with people's power, the very constituent dimension of the democratic idea. When there's no longer a fundamental difference between the programmes of right and left-wing parties, citizens think their vote won't make a difference. They feel excluded by the elites in power, and that creates a fertile ground for parties that present themselves as the voice of the people against the 'Establishment'. This is what characterises the current situation, and that's why we can say we're living in the time of post-politics in post-democratic societies.

The second thing to take into account in attempting to understand this post-political situation that deprives citizens of any possibility of political alternatives are the new forms of subordination that are connected to the development of globalised financial capitalism. This capitalism exerts its domination in a way that some call 'biopolitics', and it elicits resistances which can rarely be channelled through the existing institutions.

These transformations have created the conditions for a 'populist situation', characterised by a profound crisis of the system of representation. In that sense I agree with what you said about some degree of 'Latin-Americanisation' of Europe. This crisis manifests itself in a growing polarisation of the social arena, and in the appearance of protest movements that in some cases even question representative democracy itself. Under certain conditions, these demands can find a form of anti-system populist articulation, which in Europe can be both right- and left-wing.

ÍE: I would add that populist-type constructions appear in situations marked by two factors. The first one is the ruling groups' inability to maintain consent and integrate discontent by offering guarantees and trust to subordinate groups, as a way of broadening and reinforcing the traditional power bloc, which thus starts to erode and disaggregate. This is accompanied by a blocking of institutional channels, which are no longer able to respond to the petitions and demands they receive – because of a lack of either resources, willingness or political capacity. This opens the way for a horizontal grouping of discontent against the status quo, collapsing together the internal differences that exist within the regime. All in all, this is what we would call an organic crisis.

The second factor is that this expansion of unrest or will for change takes place in a dislocated and fragmented social arena, with no single set of unifying points of reference, narratives or group allegiances that could 'naturally' frame and guide it.

If these two conditions are met, the context is favourable for the construction of a popular identity that is able to bring together into one group all the pain and frustration, by means of a symbolic polarisation: and through this it becomes possible to construct a popular will around new or re-signified reference points, benchmarks, names and symbols, which act as its catalysts.

It is in such moments that 'populist ruptures' can take place, able to produce political change and new hegemonies. These ruptures are not, however, inevitable, as they depend on both the luck and skill of those who are defending the existing order, and on the ingenuity of those who are defying it.

CM: I also think that it's possible to speak of an 'organic crisis' in many cases, but that this in no way a guarantee of a progressive outcome to such crises. There's always the possibility that the outcome might be what you described earlier in relation to the Spanish Transition, what Gramsci calls a 'passive revolution' or 'hegemony by neutralisation':

when those in power manage to re-establish their hegemony, reclaiming and neutralising their opponents' demands.

ÍE: Why have populist situations appeared in European countries that have such obvious differences? Because there has been, I think, a collapse of the narratives and institutions of the elite groups that have until recently been distributing positions and ordering loyalties. That way of doing things has now in many cases collapsed. But it hasn't collapsed because people are out on the streets protesting against the existing order; it is because they are at home, resigned and passive, having lost all faith in representation. There has been a divorce, a separation, between representatives and represented, and an accumulation of discontent. In southern Europe – and I'm not sure if you'll agree with me here – this discontent has to do chiefly with unjust and brutal cuts and austerity measures; whereas in northern countries it is perhaps more closely related to a lack of alternatives in the political system, even when social conditions have not deteriorated to such an extent. Nevertheless – and this is a crucial point if we are to avoid a mistaken diagnosis – we are not talking here about situations of state crisis, but of regime crisis: we are at the end of a cycle, in a period that is characterised by the breakdown of the established consensus, actors and power equilibrium. This, however, has in in no way compromised the state's ability to guarantee order, or to maintain territorial control, certainty and the monopoly of violence. Understanding this is decisive for analysis, but also for political hypotheses.

CM: The conditions are different in southern and northern Europe, but I think there are nevertheless common traits that have to do with a deep crisis of representative democracy in all European countries. There has been an accumulation of demands which cannot express themselves through the existing channels.

I first noticed this crisis of representation when I became interested in the Freedom Party (FPÖ) in Austria, Jörg Haider's party. The Austrian case is particularly interesting because the ground for populism was established by the Grand Coalition between the conservatives (ÖVP) and social-democrats (SPÖ) at a time before the development of the Third Way. To have any access to a public post it was necessary to be a member of one of those parties, and many people started to feel excluded from the system. This allowed Haider to present himself as the one who could give voice to the people and reinvigorate democracy. Evidently, the parties in power accused him of populism.

ÍE: I don't think populist situations arise just anywhere, only in contexts that are heavily marked by dislocation, by the collapse of traditional identities. People feel angry and abandoned, and lack any reference points that could articulate their anger. And in the absence of such reference points, a polarisation of the political field takes place, between an ever-growing potential majority, unsatisfied with the current state of things, and the elite groups, which are perceived as being increasingly similar to each other: 'Well, there are some differences between those of you up there, but they are in the small print.' The most important difference is not between different elite groups, but between you as a group – the *casta*, as we say here – and normal citizens. This produces a polarisation, a dichotomisation, between common citizens – the people – and the elite. This situation isn't necessarily productive on its own, but it is potentially populist, in that there is a widespread feeling of abandonment, and discontent is fragmented; it is not represented in the institutions by the available political discourses. What's still missing in that situation is, I think, that moment in the chain of equivalences when the different dissatisfactions gradually federate. It's good to remember here what you said before, that these dissatisfactions might not have anything in common, but that they initially join forces through their shared frustration, because they've all been blocked by the power system. The moment of bringing together all the demands or dissatisfactions is followed by the construction of a national collective popular will.

CM: From the point of view of our discussion on populism, how do you see 15M?

ÍE: I think there were clearly populist traits in 15M, in the oppositionalist or destituent part, and in the bringing together of different demands.[10] All of a sudden, it seemed clear that there was an 'above' and a 'below' which were more important than the traditional two-party identification. Suddenly, a plethora of social themes and problems came to be lived as political, and attributed to the state of affairs we were living in, and the incapacity or selfishness of those in power – who inevitably began to age and to look defensive about the new issues that had been placed in the agenda by the mobilisations.

However, the next step never took place: the coming together of unsatisfied demands didn't crystallise into a new popular will, or didn't crystallise such popular will

10 See note 6 for discussion of the term destituent.

into consistent enduring forms, despite having created the right cultural climate for it. It didn't produce any vertical moment, or result in new political alternatives, leaderships or programmes, but there was clearly an initial moment when it produced a new primary political opposition. On one side were the citizens, and on the other the politicians and the bankers, to use the initial 15 May terms. This moment did take place, and we have since made advances in the construction of a popular identity in the non-institutional sense, which is not represented in the institutions as they are now – a new popular force. It is therefore possible to say that we're currently living with populist situations in several places in Europe, and definitely so in Spain. The crisis of the political regime of 1978, and the growth of an ambivalent and inorganic discontent, is today being articulated in a new and not-yet-represented direction, and this makes it possible to speak of a populist moment.

CM: You'd therefore agree that this populist situation in several European countries is connected to the crisis of traditional parties and their incapacity to give expression to the new antagonisms produced by neoliberalism.

ÍE: In the South it's not just the parties. The institutions too have been incapable of responding to the wide range of very urgent social demands coming from the population – and perhaps this is the most important thing. This discontent only started to pile up when institutions were no longer able to provide an answer. The replacement of politics by what is regarded as merely a system of technical management is, I think, behind the crisis of representation emerging all across Europe. But additionally, in the case of southern

Europe, in the midst of what is a severe social crisis, many people are not finding an answer in the institutions. I think our European states, as well-functioning states, managed to individualise social relations and to split civil society from political society – to guide and domesticate it and to offer certainties and comfort. This generated a social composition of 'citizens' rather than 'a people', which was reflected in political behaviour. If citizens had a problem, they were sent to counter number one for an solution; if they had a type-two problem they were sent to counter number two, and if was a type-three problem to counter number three. But then counter number one closed, and so did counters two and three, and that meant that discontent started to become politicised, to receive an expression which was more popular than institutional. While it is not inevitable that this expression of discontent should produce anything in political terms, or take a particular direction, it does enable a new division of the political field into, on the one hand, what is now seen as the old and on the other, those who offer the possibility of overcoming the old ways. However, neither the delineation of this new frontier nor the outcome of this struggle are pre-given. This is what has been happening in Spain, albeit with some traits of its own, derived from our specific political regime, its deficiencies, the social coalition on which it rests, and the democratic expansion possibilities opened by the 15M Movement. Elsewhere in Europe the coordinates of these processes might be very different.

It is possible that this type of situation might be spreading across southern Europe, although taking different forms. For instance, it might have partially manifested itself in the Five Star movement in Italy, with whom we have nothing to do ideologically, but which has also modelled a construction –

a representation, let's say – of a supposed 'common man' or 'common citizen', not represented by the traditional elites.

CM: Now you mention the Five Star movement, I'd like you to clarify the differences between Beppe Grillo's movement and Podemos, because I've noticed many people somehow equate the two.

ÍE: We've been frequently asked about those supposed similarities. I'm not an expert on Five Star, but I'd say we share with them a general political context, which we express and react to, as well as some forms of political identification construction. But, contrary to what some might think, in our case internet organisation and participation do not substitute for work on the ground or the fundamental dimension of street presence.

Another difference is the more plebeian content of our discourse – as when we denounce the political elites, the *casta*, who have liberated themselves from the citizens they should be representing. We question them not just because of their incapacity or moral turpitude, but because they put themselves at the service of the privileged: 'butlers of the rich instead of messengers of the citizens'. We subvert the left/right symbolic dimension, but replace it not with some sort of moral frontier, but with a politics of clear national-popular content: the real country, that of the majority, of those below, as opposed to those at the top; or of democracy/oligarchy in more analytical terms.

In any case, and going back to the original discussion, this return of the popular – in its different forms – has been confusing for many, as it has been relatively absent from European politics for a long time. This situation probably indicates the path that

European politics will follow, at least during the crisis years: either there will be a victory for the liberal elites, resulting from some degree of success in reordering the political map; or there will be the construction of a new popular will – which may take a progressive direction if there are political powers capable of realising it, or a reactionary one if there aren't.

CM: To me democracy necessarily has to have a partisan character. When there's no possibility of choosing between real alternatives in the ballot box, a period of substantial political apathy ensues. But this also creates the space for the emergence of parties that present themselves as capable of giving a voice to those who cannot identify with the traditional parties, and which claim to defend the interests of those excluded by the elites in power. Since *On the political*, I have insisted that the success of right-wing populist parties is due to the post-political situation. Admittedly, this situation could also favour left-wing populism, but it's notable that the latter has largely been of phenomenon of southern Europe, while elsewhere in Europe populist parties are right-wing.

ÍE: Yes, and this has to do with the centrality of social issues, with the hijacking of democracy, and the increasingly rapid deterioration of living standards. Populist mobilisations and constructions here are heavily marked by impoverishment. They are not just a reaction to a lack of representation; they also result from the fact that the vast majority of the population are living through a time of extremely rapid impoverishment, and people are in greater debt than ever. This kind of popular will construction has wealth redistribution at its heart, because it is wealth redistribution that has split our societies, and has generated this crisis – the feeling that the privileged have ignored the social contract, put themselves above the law, and accumulated more wealth than ever.

CM: But to a certain extent that has happened all across Europe: it's a consequence of the neoliberal model. It's just that the economic conditions are much more severe in the south, and people's suffering has been greater there than in northern Europe.

I would like to draw attention to the fact that this emergence in Europe of parties that construct the political frontier in 'populist' terms – as a confrontation between 'the people' and 'the establishment' – proves the relevance of Laclau's model for our societies. Those who claim that referencing his theoretical approach and adopting its categories entails the imposition of a 'Chavism' model onto European politics, do so because they are incapable of distinguishing between the analytical level that characterises political theory and the multiplicity of specific cases which those categories illuminate.

11. Charismatic leadership and the nature of representation

ÍE: An element which I think is both interesting and controversial is the issue of leadership – the need to crystallise politics into symbols, into a project for a new country, into leaderships, myths, popular expressions, songs, anniversaries and literature. All that symbolic arsenal which takes us from opposition to the construction of a new general interest, to becoming a force capable of disputing hegemony. I have a keen interest in this cultural and symbolic arsenal, which can act as the indispensable intellectual, moral, and affective glue of a new people.

CM: To turn heterogeneous demands into a collective will it's necessary to have a figure that can represent that unity, and I don't think there can be a populist moment without leadership, that's for sure. To many people, the idea of charismatic leadership seems problematic, and doubtless it can have negative effects. But that shouldn't blind us to its importance. It all depends on the type of relation that is established between the leader and the people. In the case of right-wing populism, it's a very authoritarian relation, where everything comes from the top, without real grass-roots participation. That's clearly the case with Marine Le Pen. But it doesn't have to be that way, and the way I see it, it's perfectly possible to establish a different type of relationship, less vertical, between the leader and the different groups that constitute the movement.

ÍE: I agree, and I'd even go further: it's quite possible that there could never be a construction of a general will that didn't crystallise, in one way or other, into some kind of representation involving an affective bond with a charismatic leader. In fact, I'd say – and I'm not sure if you'll agree with me here – that the level of a society's institutionalisation is negatively correlated with the importance within it of charismatic-type leaderships, because in more institutionalised societies there are more, and more efficient, institutional mediations.

CM: I would agree with that. But in highly institutionalised societies there are no populist situations.

ÍE: Agreed. But it's interesting to observe that some form of leadership phenomenon always emerges, across very different situations and political cultures. I often quote an example from Spain's anarcho-syndicalist movement, a more horizontal – and therefore in principle more hostile to leadership – political tradition: during our Civil War, hundreds of thousands of workers paid their final farewells to the anarchist leader Buenaventura Durruti at his funeral. Did they say their farewell because he had special powers, because he was magic, the Messiah, the ruler? No, they did so because his name, Durruti, had become a common name, a name that represented far more people than just himself. And this happened in a horizontal political culture, one that in principle is very hostile to representation. I think this is something we should discuss – that leadership is not a relationship of substitution, but one of representation. Because while it's true that leadership expresses a collective will that also serves as catalyst for change, it also needs to incorporate some of the desires of the represented: if it stops incorporating them, it stops being a leadership; it stops leading. So the relationship is always mainly one of representation.

This doesn't mean, however, that – as I have observed in other examples of political change – leadership doesn't entail the risk of decisionism or of crystallisation into forms (for example being closed off by entourages and minders) that can be detrimental to democracy, or to picking the best ideas. But overall, I don't think there are any forms of organisation that are exempt from those risks and deficiencies.

CM: The issue of representation seems crucial to me. I'd like to approach it through a critique of the proposition that representative democracy is an oxymoron because a true democracy can never be representative. This is a common position among those who interpret the movement of the indignados in anti-representative terms, as the manifestation of a 'presentist' democracy. To me it is evident that there can be no democracy without representation. If one accepts the theoretical approach according to which identities are never given in an essentialist manner, but always produced through a discursive construction, one must also recognise that this process of construction is a process of representation. Political subjects don't already exist, they are created through representation. Any affirmation of a political identity is therefore internal, not external, to the process of representation.

ÍE: And, in more empirical terms, there can never be a permanent direct democracy or a total continuous mobilisation or participation. Any political theory that relies on people's constant participation or mobilisation is doomed to nostalgia, to melancholy, because it never happens – people always go home. I think it's necessary to recognise that popular mobilisation has moments of ebb and flow, and that one must always build a project with the assumption that the ebb will eventually come, and an assessment of how much will have been sedimented by then, so that the advances of your time leave at least some foundations. This is the idea of relative irreversibility, on which I've been working for a while now. How can a political power create a set of conditions – in economic structure, institutions, common sense, political culture – that have to be accepted even by its opponents? And I say 'relative irreversibility' because, luckily, there's nothing fixed or permanent in politics – which is a guarantee of freedom. The advances made in periods of more intense activity are only consolidated when they are dug in and entrenched – institutionalised and made part of a new everyday, a new way of being in common. That's what the conservative neoliberal counter-revolution did in Europe – hence the difficulty of overturning it – and that was also, in a different direction, the challenge of the Latin-American popular governments.

Another time of flow will come, perhaps in three decades' time, but we always need to work on the premise that we're transitory, that conquests must be consolidated and expanded, which requires management, efficacy, and moral and intellectual reform. Otherwise, conquests depend on popular fervour and constant heroism, but that never lasts forever. That's what activist fantasies envisage, but it never happens. Any model of operation, representation and organisation that relies entirely on people's permanent participation is thus bound to disappointment – or to regret, after the inevitable appearance on to the scene of a tradition that diverts the true revolutionary potential. This is a problem which is more moral than political: after the rupture – which is never total and always inherits more from the past than at first seems to be the case – comes the recomposition, the construction of a different order. You storm the Winter Palace, but a few days or years later people always go home. The key is finding a way to ensure there is no regression, and to reconcile that with pluralism.

CM: What's important is that the mobilisation is used by people to build an identity; the fact that identities are always constructed is to me a fundamental point. The way in which the idea of representation is generally understood, as a representation of already existing identities, is completely wrong, because representation is also a process of identity constitution. In other words, there are no given identities that the party can simply represent. Politics is also about the construction of identities. There is therefore a double movement, from the represented to the representative, and from the representative to the represented.

ÍE: It represents and in doing so it constructs.

CM: Besides, in a democratic society that doesn't conceive of pluralism in a harmonious anti-political way – one in which the ever-present possibility of antagonism is taken into account – representative institutions, in giving form to social divisions, play a crucial role in the institutionalisation of this conflictual dimension. That is why representation is a condition of democratic politics, and why the idea of a 'presentist' democracy beyond representation must be abandoned. Such a conception generally goes together with the illusion that it's possible to achieve an 'absolute democracy', in which all demands are satisfied.

How do you think we should deal with the idea that demands can ever one day be satisfied or, more generally, with the messianic dimension that sometimes characterises politics? What can we do, for instance, when, as you said before, people come up to you and say you 'brother, don't fail us'?

ÍE: I think there we need to move along two tracks. The first one is that of the present – of the media discussion in which we have to play by a set of rules, and within a political culture, that have essentially been built by the adversary, and which require the production of hopes and passions. But there is also a second, parallel, track – we use the mantra 'short step and long gaze' to describe this, and the necessary conciliation between the two cycles. The first one, the short step, is necessary for taking advantage of the window of opportunity, narrow and deep, offered by the regime crisis. That window won't be open forever: powerful forces are working to narrow it, or close it off through a restoration from above. To have any influence within that window of opportunity we have to move according to the tempos and rules of the opponent – there's no point in complaining about that. But there is also the project of the longer cycle, the necessary task of popular, community, and cultural reconstruction, so as to be in a position to restore what has been destroyed by decades of neoliberal fragmentation – an effort of intellectual and moral reform, in Gramsci's terms. But the immediate political dispute runs at a faster pace, under the dictatorship of the immediate moment.

It's easy for armchair theorists to be dismissive of the terms of the immediate dispute, but, in our context, if we fail to dispute this ground, and stop the restoration, we'll have lost a crucial opportunity, and then we'll have to fight the longer battle in terrible conditions.

However, the limits of this immediate, let's say political-electoral, battle are evident. Whether we're dealing with the shaping of a new consensus or the opening of a new horizon, not all problems can be solved – or sometimes even tackled – in accordance with the tempos of official politics.

Sometimes, when we're asked to defend certain demands, we say, 'yes, but civil society also needs to construct a majority opinion that is supportive of that demand – that is not something we can do within the tempo of the immediate battle for political power'. Some things are built at a slower pace, through the work of intellectual reform that can start to shape society's perception.

And when it comes to that Messianic requirement 'don't fail us'? Well, as I was saying, this is something people repeat a lot, it's one of the most common sentences we hear. And we have an ambivalent attitude towards it. On the one hand, we understand the message and the responsibility, and we all work as hard as we can to rise to the challenge. But, on the other, we can also see the work of cultural and educational transformation that still needs to be done if we are to create the conditions in which that 'don't fail us' becomes a 'let's not fail ourselves' – to construct a popular will and an organisation capable of recovering sovereignty.

I think our political initiative must move between these two tracks, which have different paces, and two rationales that don't always coincide. On the one hand, popular articulation, and all the pressing tasks of the moment, in conditions which we haven't chosen; on the other, in parallel, a more molecular process of education and construction. Without the first, we risk missing this historical moment for our country, we live in the world of ideas. Without the second, it will be difficult to resist the powerful forces ranged against us in an enduring way. But if we win in the first set of tasks, it will be easier to create good conditions for our work towards the construction of a people.

CM: Yes, that's true. I agree with this idea of two tracks. But it's also necessary to fight against that messianic dimension that leads to the notion that there might be a final reconciliation – although it might sometimes be difficult to resist.

ÍE: We don't say that. We say we want to restore democracy – which has been hijacked by the elite and the power of finance – and that involves the battle of ideas, a never-ending struggle. We don't promise an end to all problems and conflicts, only the construction of a framework that puts them under popular sovereignty.

In terms of your theoretical question about the possibility of final resolution, it's interesting how very different roads – marxism, liberalism – lead to that same idea. Why? Because liberalism also incorporates, to some extent, the possibility of cancelling politics, or of having societies which are as empty of politics as possible. If politics means conflict, let's suspend politics. As for marxism, it envisages that there will be a time when, having abolished the fundamental contradiction –that between capital and wage labour – we'll be able to have societies which are free of politics.

CM: It's for this reason that we've insisted that our notion of the radicalisation of democracy also implies recognising the impossibility of the final realisation of democracy. A pluralist democracy requires always being able to question a given state of democratic institutions. Otherwise it's the end of politics and pluralism. In this sense, it's very important to recognise that we'll never be the 100 per cent. That's precisely what my model of agonistic democracy highlights, that democracy exists only inasmuch as there is confrontation between adversaries. In that sense, even though I recognised its capacity for mobilisation, I had issues with Occupy's 'we are the 99 per cent' slogan, because it didn't recognise the important divisions that exist in society, and the need to provide democratic channels of expression for them.

ÍE: I see this differently. I think the statement 'we are the 99 per cent' doesn't have a statistical value but a performative one: it appeals to a very heterogeneous majority united in opposition to the super-rich 1 per cent.

In any case, that's why it's so important to insist that what has put our democracies at risk hasn't been our differences, or the battle between conflicting ideas, but the gradual disappearance of any sense of a dispute between substantially different options – the feeling that nothing decisive is at stake in the competitions between elite groups, because everything has already been decided, behind closed doors and beyond the control of ordinary citizens. The privileged tend to dismiss as 'unrest' or 'polarisation' anything that signals the opening of a horizon that asks: 'could things be different?' It's not confrontation that is dangerous, but rather the impossibility of finding a political voice that can express people's pain.

CM: Yes, to me there's no doubt that the lack of an agonistic public sphere is the origin of the post-democratic situation in which our democracies find themselves.

12. Ideas of right and left

ÍE: I think it would be interesting to introduce a topic which I know is very controversial, and which might provoke a mixed response in Europe: the pertinence of the metaphors of left and right.

CM: It's definitely a topic we need to address, because many people don't understand the position of Podemos in that respect. It would be good if you could explain why you reject the left-right distinction, and why you don't want to position yourselves on that axis.

ÍE: It's not that we reject it. It exists in many societies. It's the main frontier that explains people's identifications in many parts of Europe. But we think that's not the case in Spain now. It may become so again, but currently it isn't. Anybody who believes that that division is the key for understanding what's happening in our country wouldn't understand why it is that, all of a sudden, within the space of a year, the electoral map has changed so much. What has happened? Has the left's territory greatly expanded? No, that's not what's happened. Then why has the Spanish political map changed so much? Because, by changing the questions, the answers have also changed. A change in the frontiers that order the political arena has brought about a potential change in the balance of forces, the possibility of a new vote, defined in patriotic, civic and democratic terms. That's why the elites feel such longing for the old questions, the set of ideas around which they could organise their distribution of positions, and which they could use to deactivate the formation of a potential popular alliance that could form a majority against them. I'm not talking here about a marketing operation, designed to obscure what we are, or about a renunciation of conflict. On the contrary, I'm talking about a battle over meaning which no longer confronts the old order in its own terms.

It is of course undeniable that we come, biographically, familially and personally, from the tradition and commitment of the left. I come, for instance, from a family persecuted by Francoism, my father was a political prisoner. Yet we still say that left and right are not the main frontier for producing political change in Spain. But that's not because of an electoral public relations exercise, or political pragmatism. We are not keeping something secret, or putting forward a new story in order to hide our true essence, disguising it as something else in order to run for election. In conservative circles they believe that they can discover the hidden truth of Podemos by delving into our past – they haven't understood a thing about what's going on in Spain. It's not about that at all. It's about recognising, firstly, that political positions are not given, that political identities are not stable: there is nothing natural about people identifying as right or left; that is something that is historically and geographically contingent. And secondly, it's about recognising that there have been transformations in our country that in our view have produced a hijacking of democracy by the oligarchy. This allows for the postulation of a frontier that is defined in theoretical terms as democracy/oligarchy, and in more tangible terms as citizens/privileged or *casta*. This is better able to explain the crisis we – and the 1978 political map – are undergoing. In these terms it is no longer the elite that determines our political vocabulary or the distribution of positions: they have to move defensively, having lost public respect, and become separated from citizens.

CM: I completely agree that in recent years there has been an oligarchic hijack of democracy. It has happened across Europe, not just in Spain, but it has taken different forms. It's a sign of the 'Latin-Americanisation' of Europe we were talking about before. To me it's a consequence of neoliberalism, and that is why it's accurate to say that we are living in 'post-democratic' societies. Furthermore, the consensus at the centre that we discussed previously has contributed to the discrediting of left-wing politics. How has that manifested itself in Spain?

ÍE: I think it manifested itself in the lack of any alternatives to the Socialist Party that had hegemonic capacity or intention. For a long time, the Socialist Party was capable of capturing the significant forces of the left, to the extent that the erosion of each of them has gone hand in hand. To be left-wing in

Spain was to support the Socialist Party, and the decline of the Socialist Party has been the decline of the left. At a certain point, part of the left decided they had to fight for the truth of the word 'left': 'we're the true left'. But from the beginning we said 'you can keep it, we hand it over to you. We're interested in constructing a people, not in constructing the left'.

CM: I understand that position and I agree with the idea that we must establish the frontier in a different way. I also think it's necessary to build a citizen collective will, a people. But I think we need to clarify how we want to build it. It's not enough to oppose the people to the *casta*. You could not approach things in the same way if you were in France, where there is a right-wing populist movement that also constructs a cross-cutting frontier of people/elites, albeit differently. If you were facing a Marine Le Pen, you couldn't just say, 'we are the people'.

ÍE: We don't say it directly either, because the people don't have a legitimate representative, precisely because they're neither homogeneous nor pre-exist their construction, which is always new. It's a rhetorical battle. But, clearly, we do appeal to a wider constituency – because current conditions allow us to do so, and because we have hegemonic and state aspirations. There is today a majority of citizens, non-homogeneous but relatively transversal, which as a group feels cheated and unrepresented, and wants to reclaim the institutions – and now has the means to do so. We aspire to be that means, while also knowing that the road ahead is difficult, and most often it's the powerful who win. That approach has certainly been controversial, and I'm not sure how it's read and interpreted from abroad. But the progressive and democratic character of our popular construction derives from who it is that we identify as adversary, and precisely from the recognition of the contingency and the pluralism of the people.

CM: Outside of Spain you are seen as a left party, and even though I think asking whether you are right- or left-wing is not the most pertinent question for understanding Podemos, I don't see why you have such difficulties in accepting that label. I know it's not your position, but there is a risk that the rejection of any reference to the right/left frontier might be interpreted as an acceptance of the Third Way position, according to which politics must be thought beyond right and left.

ÍE: It's true that saying 'we must subvert the left and right frontier' has generated much mistrust amongst progressive groups. It's been understood as if we were saying that ideologies were no longer valid, or as some sort of extreme pragmatism. One can agree or disagree with our hypothesis, but that interpretation is wrong. We've said that if identities are constructed, and if that construction is always done through frontiers, a different frontier can draw a new alternative popular majority which wasn't there before. The elite were very comfortable with the left-right axis. They located themselves at the centre-right/centre-left, and placed the 'challengers' – those who defied them – at the margins. But if we draw a cross-cutting citizens-*casta* frontier, all of a sudden they are confused; they are out of their comfort zone, finding themselves in a very uncomfortable political and symbolic arena. In fact – and thereby nicely demonstrating a certain exhaustion of their capacity for political imagination – the people who have traditionally monopolised politics have had to accept there is something called *casta*: their best defence has not been to shake off the accusation, but to attempt to smear us as well – as if they recognise that they can never be likeable, but hope that, for them to stay in power, it will be enough to extend that mistrust to us – to discourage change and reinstall cynicism. That is a symptom of an intellectual crisis, but in no way a negligible strategy, especially if we take into account the powerful media and many resources in their hands.

CM: It's true that with the rise of the Third Way we've reached a situation where the traditional right/left axis no longer constitutes a frontier. The question now is to know whether we need to reactivate it or should abandon it altogether to construct a new one.

ÍE: The Third Way has that consensual call of 'there's no longer any frontiers, there's only management and technical differences'. We don't say there aren't any differences, or that there are no ideologies. We replace one frontier with another one, above/below, which I think is in fact more radical in the best sense of the term. With the left-right frontier, the cards are comfortably dealt by the traditional actors, who place themselves at the centre of the distribution of positions. With a citizenry-*casta* frontier, however, they are suddenly forced to play on a very difficult terrain. I think it's important to explain this to other Europeans, so it doesn't seem as if there has been some sort of renunciation of ideological confrontation, or a belief that there can be a democracy without differences.

An anti-essentialist view allows us to understand that to aspire to subvert or cut across the metaphors of right and left is not a renunciation of ideologies, but a different way of presenting a dispute for meaning. That allows us to construct a different set of political meanings, directed towards the formation of a different general will. There is nothing essential, nothing necessary, in the terms right and left as metaphors around which to structure the political arena. In my opinion, they are useful or not depending on whether or not they can be used to construct a balance of power that is more favourable to the subaltern.

13. Towards a left-wing populism?

CM: I agree, but to build a collective will that is capable of realising a progressive agenda it is not enough to build a people/*casta* frontier, as if the people were necessarily in favour of promoting equality. The success of right-wing populism demonstrates that is not the case. To me, the crucial question here is how to propound a form of politics aimed at the radicalisation of democracy. I imagine that you might not agree with me on this point, but my position is that a contemporary project for the radicalisation of democracy requires the development of a 'left-wing populism'. For a long time I thought that in order to fight the post-political trend and create the conditions for an agonistic confrontation that would enable us to radicalise democracy, it was necessary to give new validity to the right/left frontier. But then I started to realise that in the current conditions this wasn't the appropriate path, and that it was necessary to establish the frontier in a different way – through the construction of a collective will that is transversal and progressive, and capable of defying the new oligarchic forms that have resulted from neoliberalism. That's what I call 'left-wing populism'. I reached this conclusion for the following reasons.

Firstly, I realised that most centre-left parties had been too closely involved in neoliberal hegemony to be reformable – having in many cases even contributed to its installation. From the time of the crisis of 2008 it became evident that they were accomplices in the austerity policies that were imposed to defend that order, and that it was illusory to think they could ever change their line to the point of defying the neoliberal order. The 'consensus at the centre' would not allow the reactivation of an agonistic confrontation along the right/left axis. In a way, it's something Beck and Giddens already saw, but to them it represented progress. Their conclusion was that there were no longer any antagonisms and they celebrated the advent of politics without frontiers.

But there is another reason why the traditional right/left frontier cannot be used to radicalise democracy, and it has to do with the transformations resulting from the new mode of regulation of capitalism. In the era of neoliberal globalisation and the financialisation of capitalism, new antagonisms have emerged, derived from the subjugation of all social life to the empire of the market. Today one is not subject to capitalist logic only through labour; its requirements affect the life of the individual in all its aspects. Furthermore, levels of inequality between the oligarchic financial powers and the rest of society have greatly increased. The usual categories of left politics cannot account for this wide range of forms of subordination, or for the new oligarchy of the super-rich. It's necessary to conceive the struggle in different terms from those used by both social democracy and marxism. This is something that theorists of the multitude like Hardt and Negri to a certain extent recognise, but they do so based on an analysis of the evolution of capitalism which I find problematic. Furthermore, what's missing from their approach is any acknowledgement of the need to articulate the multiplicity of heterogeneous struggles into a collective will, into 'a people'; or the need to work with institutions to achieve the establishment of a new hegemony.

I think that when one takes into account all these political and economic changes, it becomes clear that if we are to create the conditions for an agonistic hegemonic struggle against the neoliberal order and bring an end to post-politics in Europe, we must implement a type of politics capable of giving form to those new kinds of conflict. The goal must be to establish a chain of equivalences between the multiplicity of democratic demands, and an alliance that is able to question the existing order and build a new hegemony. That requires establishing a dialogue with a variety of struggles and institutional forms. We need a synergy between electoral competition and the wide range of struggles that take place in the social arena. It's clear that the democratic demands that exist in our societies cannot find an expression solely through the vertical party form, that they also need horizontal forms of expression. A new form of political organisation that articulates the two modes – that's how I conceive 'left-wing populism'. Clearly, however, that response will have to be concretised in different ways depending on the specific circumstances of the different European countries – this is not about imposing a single modality.

ÍE: It all depends on the arena we're working in. In the intellectual arena, there is now a form of political construction in Spain that could be described as populist (provided we strip the term of the pejorative and anti-democratic connotations that are characteristic of the loose way it is used in the dominant discourse). But at the same time, we're also intervening politically, and to do so we cannot use a term that has been cursed by the media. Nobody with any pretension to win at some point can accept a definition which in the collective imaginary immediately is taken to mean demagogy.

CM: I understand, but we shouldn't accept the semantic field the adversaries try to impose on us. We must defend a different view of populism, like the one we discussed earlier in relation to Ernesto Laclau's analytical conception in *On Populist Reason*. When I talk about left-wing populism I refer to a form of politics conceived as war of position, and the construction of collective popular will through chains of equivalence and the mobilisation of passions. Thus conceived, 'left-wing populism' allows the establishment of a difference with the centre-left or far-left, as well as with right-wing populist parties.

ÍE: I agree – but try to explain those theories in a TV studio, in three minutes and with seven people shouting at you. It's impossible. Thus, it's a valid concept for reflective analysis, for intellectual analysis, but it is not so useful in the front line of media discussion.

I wrote an article for the French edition of *Le Monde Diplomatique* that uses the term. In that context, you can qualify it, you can explain it, it can be used. But when you only have the chance to say one sentence, it's not useful. Not because of any attempt to hide something, but because the term has two usages. In Spain's media language it has become synonymous with lying and demagogy: so who is going to willingly adopt such a label?

CM: It's precisely because of this that I insist on the importance of re-appropriating the term populism. That it is being used in a derogatory way by parties who defend the status quo is no reason to abandon it. It's necessary to reclaim it, to resignify it, and to give it a positive meaning with the notion of 'left-wing populism'.

ÍE: That's for the medium term. It cannot be done in three months. But yes, it is possible. The most useful thing here, however, is to think about why the word has come back. Why is it now being used by the elite? You said the other day, anything that defies the notion that 'there is no alternative' is immediately dismissed as populist. At a time of the greatest ever concentration of power and wealth at the top of the pyramid, and when popular sovereignty is least discernible, any alternative that questions the status quo is branded as populist. This can be seen as a mirror – a mirror reflecting the elite: the less they can tolerate the 'people', the more they define you as populist.

CM: The answer should be: 'Yes we're populist because we are democrats, and there's necessarily a populist dimension in any democracy that aims to build a *demos*, a people. And we're also left-wing populists because our objective is to radicalise democracy'. Is there anything wrong with that? You said just now that the future path of European politics will depend on the elite's capacity to redraw the map, and on the constitution of popular wills – whether progressive or a reactionary. I agree with that, and I'm convinced that the fundamental political struggle in Europe in the coming years will be between right-wing and left-wing populisms. The key issue here is how the people is built, from what chain of equivalence. Is it going to be a right-wing or a left-wing people? It's not enough to say one will give voice to the people, as if its identity was already given. That's why we need to explain what sort of people we want to build. In politics one always needs to choose sides. You had to do it when you got to the European Parliament. By the way, it could seem somehow inconsistent to refuse to identify with the left and at the same time be part of the radical left group in the European Parliament, together with *Die Linke*, the *Front de Gauche*, Syriza, and other radical organisations. Syriza literally means 'party of the radical left' and Tsipras has no problems in identifying as left.

ÍE: That's because in Greece traditional organisations and identities didn't collapse; they still have powerful unions and political organisations. In Greece traditional political identities have not suffered the erosion that those in Spain have suffered. When people have been hit by adjustment policies that impoverish them, they've become angry and have taken the streets to protest. There they had traditional channels capable of articulating the protest. The left's narrative was still available and not so eroded by the growing discontent. As for the European Parliament: who could we be with otherwise? We've always defended the decision in patriotic terms.

In fact, we're in the group with Tsipras and Syriza, which are the only patriotic force that has defended the interests of the people and citizens of their country against international speculators. It's a left that has put together an inclusive project for the country. This is not something new. In *The Tailor of Ulm*, Lucio Magri describes well the best national-popular streak of the PCI, but also its deficiencies and limitations. In fact, if we look at the last Greek campaign, that which put Syriza in government, we saw a lot more 'homeland' and

'Greek people' than 'left', and they explicitly asked for the vote of those coming from the defeated centre-right parties. They didn't ask people to vote left, but to vote patriotically. That's why they've been able to reach an understanding with an anti-austerity party from the centre-right, because it's a patriotic agreement in defence of Greek sovereignty against international financial powers. That is today's most relevant political frontier in the semi-colonised countries of southern Europe. If progressive forces don't hegemonise it, either the reactionary forces will do it for us, or the liberal or social-liberal will disperse them.

Other political experiences have been important to us. We talked earlier on about Latin America – experiences of progressive advance that didn't express themselves through the left-right axis. In fact, almost none of the great processes of historical transformation have articulated around the rhetorical poles of left/right.

CM: Yes, it's true, but those Latin American experiences cannot be directly transferred, because the historical contexts and political experiences are different. The national-popular governments in South America don't have to confront right-wing populist parties. Their opponents are the oligarchies and their allies, and, in a different way, the parties that advocate a traditional conception of the left. In Europe the situation is not the same, and it's necessary to distinguish between right-wing and left-wing populisms.

Another difference has to do with what we've called the 'populist situation', which doesn't appear in the same way in Europe and South America. For the national-popular regimes in South America, the key question was how to integrate the popular sectors, previously excluded from power by the oligarchies, into the democratic project. With the exception of Argentina – where thanks to Peronism there had been a first experience of popular integration – the people had been marginalised by the elites. In Europe, however, we've had several experiences of bourgeois hegemony, in which governments somehow managed to integrate popular sectors into politics. That integration is today in crisis, but there are still loyalty bonds between parts of the people and the elites. That requires a counter-hegemonic struggle able to disarticulate those bonds and to construct a leftist people. I don't think we can take for granted that people are naturally opposed to 'the *casta*'.

14. The people/casta confrontation

ÍE: I completely agree, it has to be constructed. Again, we're in the domain of the performative rather than the descriptive. In fact 'people' only becomes meaningful when it has an 'outside' that politicises the term, if there is a 'them'.

About the possibility of national-popular ideas in Spain or southern Europe, it's obvious we're not talking about a Latin-American context – fortunately for us. We're talking about very different economic, institutional and geopolitical contexts. Perhaps the main difference is the existence of a state – even when it's one under threat of appropriation by the privileged and thus has withdrawn from some sectors – as opposed to its non-existence and the historical task of building it, as was the case in Latin America. The degree of impoverishment and social destruction caused by neoliberal policies is also, fortunately for us, very different. In Spain, a great many of the social mobilisations are 'conservative' in character, in the sense that they seek to stop financial despotism from squandering our collective assets and common wealth, and to defend our – weak – social state, public services, and security for the working-class majority.

The political moment does, however, share with Latin America the loss of credibility of those in power, and a crisis of representation and bloc disaggregation, the blocking of institutional channels, and the expansion of an inorganic discontent. This is an identifiable set of political similarities, even though it clearly operates with very different raw materials and contexts. Without the analysis of how exceptional situations such as these open up unprecedented possibilities, we would have never launched the 'Podemos' hypothesis, and we'd still be at the impasse that currently characterises many of the forces with transformative aspirations across Europe.

As you pointed out earlier, however, it's crucial to recognise that in the Spanish case there is a major current that is not so much concerned with total breakup or disengagement from the state, but which instead demands the fulfilment of the promises and guarantees that formerly held us together as a society. It has more a question of citizen dissatisfaction than of a popular attack on established power. That means the imaginable outcomes have less to do with a general contestation, and more with an opening of an institutional transformation process at the state level. This is a process which – beyond the vagaries of electoral fortune, and the possibilities they may or may not offer – will involve more a 'war of position' than a 'war of manoeuvre', in Gramscian terms.

Does this allow us to affirm the construction of a united people, and the elimination of reactionary danger? That is never guaranteed. But there is a greater threat in other European countries than there is here. In our case, the only potential authoritarianism is of the financial and technocratic kind – that's the real threat to democracy and rights in Spain. In any case, in our denomination of the people we've always defined a boundary which, while not agonistic, is definitely antagonistic. To us, the enemy, the adversary that has hijacked democracy, is those above, not those below, regardless of the country they may have come from, or their skin colour – and with people who think in that way there's no negotiation or discussion, that's an impassable frontier for us.

CM: That's a point we need to discuss. When you talk about an impassable frontier – where is it located, exactly? I think we need to clarify these notions of enemy and adversary. To me the *casta*/people confrontation is agonistic inasmuch as it takes place in the field of representative democracy, and it doesn't seek to end with the *casta* through a revolution or a coup d'état. That doesn't mean there isn't an antagonistic relationship between the opponents, it means it's an antagonism that expresses itself in an agonistic form. That is, it recognises the opponents' right to defend their point of view through elections. That's where the difference between enemy and adversary lies. The adversary is a 'legitimate enemy' which one aims to defeat, but in a way that respects democratic institutions. The agonistic struggle is a battle for hegemony; that's how I see the people/elites confrontation, which is central to the way I conceive the leftist popular identity.

ÍE: I was referring to antagonism – of the friend/enemy kind – towards reactionary, racist, and anti-democratic forces. Because, as you say, democracy also has an 'outside'. But when it comes to our political adversaries – the traditional forces of the regime and the oligarchic powers who've benefited from their programme of pillage and impoverishment – we seek to defeat them in a political battle, which, ultimately, doesn't have a definitive end. In this open, adversarial and pluralist competition, we seek to seize from the privileged minority the chance to embody the public interest, because we think they are harming Spanish democracy and the living conditions of the Spanish people, and leading us to a poorer, weaker, less democratic and more unjust country.

CM: By the way, a moment ago, when you said 'those above' – who are those above? Who is the *casta*?

ÍE: The term's mobilising power comes precisely from its lack of definition. It's like asking: who's the oligarchy? Who's the people? They are statistically undefinable. I think these are the poles with greatest performative capacity. The other day, Oxfam announced that since the beginning of the crisis, Spain has reached a situation we haven't seen in thirty years, in which 1 per cent of the Spanish population owns as much as the bottom 70 per cent. It's not about choosing a statistical marker and saying, 'you are *casta*, you are not'; what the term does is delineate a type of political construction and identification which groups a new majority, one which until then has been subaltern. There is clearly a privileged minority who have done better than everybody else and benefited from others doing worse – people who've hijacked and privatised the institutions for their own benefit, who've set up all the institutional apparatus so that it works to the benefit of the few and at the expense of the many. To reclaim democracy is to politically defeat that adversary, the privileged. It's an adversary that, despite being a social minority, has managed to construct political identifications from which to govern.

The Popular Party in Spain, for instance, has for a long time been able to speak as if it embodied the economic public interest. It's a party that has openly handed over public management and major national resources to a small group of oligarchic families, and yet it has successfully managed to present itself as being representative of the interests of small and medium-size enterprises, as the party of the small business owner. This is a hegemonic operation which we're now trying to disarticulate, so that we can articulate things differently. This is an adversary that, despite being a privileged minority, has for a long time managed to become a political majority. It therefore has to be politically defeated, but its existence and participation in the competition are, of course, legitimate.

CM: Agreed, but that's precisely why I say that the people/*casta* confrontation is agonistic, not antagonistic, in nature. It's a struggle for hegemony that takes place by means of a war of position.

In relation to that people/*casta* confrontation, I must say that I find slightly problematic when you speak of '*gente*' to refer to the people.[11] I understand it can be a comfortable term in day-to-day language, but if one thinks in terms of the formation of a collective will constituted through a chain of equivalence, speaking of *gente* doesn't seem very appropriate. I also find problematic your reference to 'people's common sense' as if that wasn't the result of a discursive construction. It smells of essentialism, and I think is in contradiction with the theoretical perspective you defend.

11 In Spanish there's two separate words for the English term 'people': *gente*, which means 'people' in its day-to-day usage and '*pueblo*', which refers to 'the people' in the political sense of the term.

ÍE: In relation to the appeal to 'common sense' – it's not done from any essentialist illusion. We're perfectly aware that such a thing doesn't exist, in fixed form, anywhere; that it results from a contestation between different discourses, and is always fluid and ambivalent; that its strength relies in its flexible capacity to present certain ideas as self-evident. It's a terrain of dispute, not a factual matter. Today, however, a good deal of existing common sense is in contradiction with the plans of the elite, and their acceptance of the adjustment programmes imposed by the Troika and other acts of financial despotism. This has placed those in power to a certain extent outside the common sense of their time – which incidentally was positively modified by the cycle opened by 15M – when it comes to subjects such as working conditions, evictions or public health. That's something we need to take advantage of, we need to reclaim the 'good sense' of the people, for we may be in an apparently paradoxical situation in which the contest between these different kinds of common sense becomes a frontier of change – in a time in which radical politics are the politics of common sense.

With respect to the terms that invest the 'us' with hegemonic capacity, I think it all depends on what 'them' they are opposed to, as it's in this clash that they become loaded with meaning. Maybe we need to be less dogmatic with regards to the terms that signify 'us'.

As I told you the other day, one time when I was giving a talk about Podemos at the University of Vienna, the translator was struggling to translate *pueblo* and *gente*. This prompted a very interesting discussion about their own problems with the term *volk* in German, which, as you know better than me, is very problematic. My response, in terms of political rather than theoretical intervention, was that naming and the hegemonic constituency can work through different words, as long as they are not already securely pinned down by the powerful, and can be used to designate a new popular will of universal reach.

While I don't know enough about the Austrian and German political and cultural system to get involved in that theoretical discussion, the bottom line is the same: the need for a careful analysis of the cultural and semantic cracks in which you can locate the counter-hegemonic project. I think it's more important to pay attention to the modes of articulation than to copy words from one experience to another.

CM: Yes, I know in Germany and Austria they have a problem with *das Volk* and many people try to use *die Bevölkerung* – the population – instead. I've had many discussions about that there, but I always argue against it and insist that it doesn't seem appropriate, because 'the population' is not a political concept.

ÍE: The population is not a political concept?

CM: No, population is a sociological concept that refers to an aggregation of individuals.

ÍE: But if it had an 'outside', if it had a 'them', it would be one, wouldn't it?

CM: I don't see how you could imagine an 'outside' of population. What would be the 'them'? It's not a type of distinction that can be used in a political way to establish a frontier.

ÍE: I understand, but in Spain *'gente'* didn't use to be one either … and yet, now it's operating as a political concept.

When we write on a sticker or poster *'es la hora de la gente'* [It's the time of people] and it's a successful appeal, which says something to people and mobilises them: what makes it a political concept? – the fact that we've drawn an 'outside', that it isn't all-embracing and empty. No, not everybody is 'common people', unentitled, those who need be united to change things. In that sense, and even though it might sound harsh, the rhetorical construction establishes a difference: there's *gente* and then there's *casta*. What I mean to say is that it used to be an amorphous and empty term, but it has now become part of a polarity, because we've defined it in terms of an outside. This helps to understand the issue of signifiers and how discourse constructs meaning and political identifications.

CM: Well, I'm ready to accept that *gente* can work as a political concept, but why don't you use terms like *pueblo* or *ciudadanía* [citizenry] instead?

ÍE: We oscillate between *ciudadanía*, *pueblo*, and *gente*. *Pueblo* sounds somewhat archaic in Spanish political language, and Francoism used it for a long time as a homogeneous will that doesn't need parties to represent it. It's thus a term that comes out during mobilisations, in moments of great political emotion, but it's not commonly used. *Ciudadanía* works quite well but is 'softer'; it certainly has less epic connotations, and until recently – although that might be changing now – it has been more anchored to the institutional discourse. In any case, it's a term in dispute, a dispute which is by no means unimportant. I maintain that *ciudadanía* can be reclaimed as a central point in a republican discourse (republican in terms of political theory, not just in relation to the Head of State), one that reconciles the popular with the institutional and its responsibility in times of change.

CM: I understand your point of view, but you can say 'the Spanish *pueblo*' but not 'the Spanish *gente*'.

ÍE: No, you would say '*la gente de este país*' [the people of this country]. 'It's high time the people of this country had a government at their service and not at the service of the privileged' – I've said that thousands of times. *Ciudadanía* works when discussing strategy. For instance, in the strategy document for the local elections, we said '*construir candidaturas de unidad popular y ciudadana*' [building candidacies of popular and citizen unity]; we united the two concepts, as there is a popular and collective component to the campaign, but also a component of outraged but more individualised citizens. I think the modernisation and institutionalisation processes have been successful in creating citizens and deconstructing 'the people'. That is, it has created a society of individualised citizens, and it's probably those we address the most. Thus, *ciudadanía* is our most commonly used term, the one that's seen as most normal, because it also has a civic-democratic republican component (in the political theory sense, not in terms of state form), which works very well, but it only works because it has an outside. That is, the point is not that the concept *ciudadanía* works very well, the point is that it works because it has *casta* – or oligarchy – on the other side.

I think we've been very undogmatic in our use of terms: we've tested them, and seen which terms could mobilise or articulate which type of interests and desires. This all turns on a crucial question for us: how to read particular cultural contexts – their consensuses, their cracks – and how to elaborate strategies adapted to each specific condition. In this case, it is through a careful consideration of the construction of meanings on which hegemony and its floating signifiers rest.

CM: In the hegemonic struggle to re-articulate the key signifiers we must always take into account the adversary's response. In the case of Podemos it's clear that they're not only doing everything in their power to delegitimise and discredit you, but they are also to trying to copy some of your proposals, while draining them of their subversive character. Could you say that they are, in a typically transformist way, trying to use the emergence of Podemos to rejuvenate themselves? How do you see that possibility?

ÍE: We shouldn't underestimate the capacity of a well-settled regime, even a worn-out one, for recovering the initiative and restoring trust. We are speaking of a regime, that of 1978, that is based on a generational story that still commands important loyalties among the oldest sectors of the population, especially in the less populated provinces (which, thanks to an electoral system expressly designed for this purpose, have more political weight). This is a regime that has built intellectual and media structures that until recently have defined what could or could not have a public existence, that has a well-oiled civil society, and that has at its disposal the plentiful resources of effective public administration and economic power. It's not a good idea to underestimate the adversary. In fact, it is rather exceptional for the powerful to see their hegemony threatened like this. Their anxiety, despite the modesty of the challenge, speaks clearly of how unaccustomed they are to being challenged.

There's certainly plenty of possibilities for a strategy that seeks both to sustain the old actors, despite their weakening power, and at the same time to revivify and broaden the 'party of order' – as Gramsci called it – through the incorporation of 'new' content and new faces. The traditional actors have learnt that they must no longer look like themselves. In this crisis of the party system, it may even be possible for some proponents of conservative regeneration to gain traction, if they present themselves as a replacement – seeking to hegemonise the criticisms of 'politicians', while ignoring the role of the privileged minority and the economic power that our representatives have been serving. We wouldn't be facing a hegemonic power if it simply rejected the new, if it didn't have some capacity to listen, learn and adapt, and to incorporate-deactivate criticisms.

CM: In relation to the monarchy, what's your position?

ÍE: Well, it isn't as decisive a question in Spanish politics as people abroad think. It's important, and we've said 'we're a democratic force, and therefore a democratic country should ...'

CM: But have you ever thought of holding a referendum?

ÍE: Yes, of course. When the monarchic succession took place, in June 2014 – largely driven, I think, by the will to reform in anticipation of an uncertain year – we said 'we're a democratic force and that means that in a country of mature citizens, the Head of State should be somebody elected by citizens – anything else is medieval'.[12] I don't think that's a central issue for political change in Spain. But something that might be is the potential role of the monarchy in safeguarding the old balance of power. In the discussion about the succession, we clearly saw the need, the intention, of the most conservative sections of elite to return to the framework of the Republic-Monarchy debate. Why? Because that would take the discussion back to the memory of the Spanish Civil War – a scenario which would allow the elite to block political discussion. This is a scenario that scares the elderly, and which doesn't mean so much to the young, as it happened a long time ago. While we're clear on what side we'd take in such an argument, we also know that nostalgia doesn't win battles, but that defeats unfortunately do build defeat. This is not an appeal to bury the whole subject, it's an appeal to fight within the terms of the time, and in the best conditions for building a new majority that sees the current cycle as closed – though not as historically invalid – with everything that that involves.

The words which the adversary wants to use and the ones we want to use are quite probably the most useful indicator of where the battle lines of meaning, of political confrontation, currently are. What the adversary wants, what it needs to talk about, and conversely, what terms we want to discuss. That 'we' is not a party-based 'we', it refers to all those sectors that haven't felt represented. It's interesting to note that when 15M started, in the first camps in Puerta del Sol, right-wing journalists asked people there about their position on terrorism, and people replied: 'what are you talking about, I'm against it, but

12 King Juan Carlos, whose reign began in 1975 as part of the new constitution, abdicated in June 2014 and was succeeded by his son Felipe.

what I'm talking about here is how I want to have the right to a home, and to have a decent job'.

The old elites needed to take the political discussion back to the topics they could still use to articulate a majority. Even when those topics were no longer on the agenda, they had to put them back on it, because only by doing so they could still represent a broad majority. That's something we constantly have to confront: the need on the part of the regime and its actors to take the topics that worry Spanish people the most out of circulation; their need to move the discussion into places where fear will allow them to deactivate the urge for change.

CM: Is the monarchy a topic that doesn't particularly interest people? Isn't there a debate about it?

ÍE: Not much, I think. There is a part of the left that is very interested in it, but it's not the central topic. It's been a while since people really discussed the institution. Opinion polls make sure not to ask about it either. Thus, I am not sure. I think they conducted a very good operation, and included some components of passive revolution, in the sense that they asked themselves: 'what are people asking for? renovation? Good, then let's change the king to save and strengthen the monarchy. We'll install this king, who is young, and not suspected of corruption'. It was a relatively successful operation that renovated the image without touching the institution. In any case, it's not something that is central to Podemos discussion.

15. Chains of equivalence and the construction of a people

CM: Going back to the issue of right/left, which I see as central to our discussion, I wonder if we shouldn't distinguish between different uses of that distinction. There is a use linked to the existence of parties which can be expressed as a horizontal axis. Its origin lies in a conception of politics as the representation of the interests of relatively homogenous sociological groups by different parties; from which one would expect a political performance corresponding to those interests. This is a perspective which may prompt very essentialist interpretations, but that doesn't necessarily have to be the case. For this horizontal-axis distinction to be politically pertinent and allow an us/them confrontation, it requires the existence of groups with relatively homogeneous interests, and a real ideological confrontation between right and left, which has virtually disappeared in a time of consensus at the centre. That's the reason why many people feel increasingly less represented by those positions. In that sense, I would agree that it's a distinction which has lost its validity to establish an agonistic political frontier.

But there is another sense of the notion of left which I think is still relevant: that which corresponds to the axis opposing those below and those above. *Gente* as opposed to *casta*, as you say. It's a different type of frontier which can be constructed in very different ways. In actuality, it's much more flexible than any conception based on socio-economic interests. That's why in this case it's so important how the 'us', 'the people', is constructed, because some constructions can be clearly harmful to democracy.

143

Incidentally, any frontier entails forms of exclusion, and seeing who is excluded is a key criterion for assessing the progressive character of the 'us'. To me, the fundamental difference between right- and left-wing populisms lies in the nature of the chains of equivalence by which the people is constructed. It's because of these different ways of constructing the people as a collective will that I think the reference to the left cannot be abandoned, as it carries notions of social justice and radicalisation of democracy. Sure, one could use another word, but if we accept Norberto Bobbio's view that the central connotation of this notion of left is the idea of equality, I think it remains central to the political struggle and should be kept. Thus, instead of abandoning valuable terms for the political struggle because you don't like the way in which they are being used, I think you should be fighting to resignify them. It's an important part of the hegemonic struggle of disarticulation-rearticulation.

ÍE: That's an intellectual doubt I always have, an ever present tension: to build new terms and symbols or to resignify existing ones? Ultimately, terms are always resignified, as there are no virgin terms; what I'm referring to is the balance between a word's sedimented meaning and its possibilities for alternative construction.

I think it's a tension that cannot be resolved in the abstract or in a laboratory, outside any context; it is one that unfolds through a trial-error dynamic, through people testing, considering and discarding terms, and proposing new ones as they confirm their power to explain what is happening and to aggregate people around that explanation.

I understand what you're saying about the value of the term 'left', but the movement for the emancipation of the dispossessed, through equality and democracy, so that nobody is seen as being of more value than anybody else, or has to live with fear, is much older than the term 'left', and also exists in societies where the symbolic axis of European parliamentarism isn't the one that defines loyalties. I don't have any problem in recognising a part of this tradition, it's in my DNA, but the plebeian 'red thread' is more heterogeneous and has been constructed with different names.

CM: There's no doubt that the term 'left' belongs to a particular tradition and that in other contexts other names are used to refer to the emancipation of the dispossessed. But you live in Spain and have to operate from the central signifiers of the European tradition. That's why I think the hegemonic struggle to resignify the notion of left is important.

From that perspective, an issue which I think is crucial is that of the chains of equivalence we've previously mentioned. We agree that to constitute a people it's necessary to articulate a wide range of heterogeneous demands which do not necessarily coalesce, and which might even be in conflict with one another. That's the key difference between the idea of people and that of multitude, for, according to Hardt and Negri, the latter doesn't require a political articulation. To establish a true collective will with hegemonic aspirations it's necessary to transform the identities of those who are going to enter the chain of equivalence, to create new subjectivities.

It's a complex process that can have several stages. An important step is to define a common adversary, a 'them' that ensures the unity of the 'us', but that's not enough in a hegemonic perspective. As has been seen in many cases – in the countries of the ex-socialist bloc, for instance, but also in the

Arab 'revolutions' – once the enemy is defeated the fight starts amongst the groups that initially united against it.

Admittedly, in those cases it was a friend/enemy type struggle, rather than an agonistic one between adversaries. In agonistic struggles, in order to ensure their success (their capacity to not just bring down a government, but also establish a new hegemony), it's necessary to build a true collective will. That requires what Gramsci calls a moral and intellectual reform, which to him means a profound transformation of common sense and of the forms of subjectivity. Only in this way will we be able to secure the chain of equivalence between heterogeneous demands. What stage are you in? The first one, where the movement is united by the common rejection of the *casta*?

ÍE: I think we're already one step beyond what you describe. There is a certain chain of equivalence, born largely from the cycle opened by 15M, and their 'they don't represent us' – which, although not a new slogan, only became widespread from then. There has been a crystallisation of that chain into certain reference points – mostly about leadership, but also about symbols and milestones. The hope of victory has played a key role in this – after the impasse in the protest cycle that could have led to demoralisation – and this has also made us leave behind certain discussions about the finer points and sectarian differences. The frenzied reaction of the powerful has also simplified the political field, making the options clearer. All of this has already happened, but we're still a few steps away from becoming a general will, or a will with hegemonic capacity, in a project for the country capable of becoming a state. But we're no longer talking about pure rejection, we've gone beyond the bringing together of a range of discontent and feelings of opposition.

CM: But is there a collective will, even in embryonic form?

ÍE: I'd say timidly so. It has reference points, leadership, vocabulary; it has milestones – or is starting to have them. It's beginning to have a project for the country, though this has to be strengthened with the incorporation of general and group experiences from many civil and professional sectors. All of that must happen simultaneously and in a hurry, under the constant fire of the adversary. We need to build ourselves organisationally, and through the aggregation of crucial electoral contests – quite a challenge in these vertiginous times. When in May 2014 we had an unexpected result in the European elections – 1,250,000 votes and 5 MEPs – a new phase began. Until then we had struggled to make ourselves visible, to become a block of contestation – albeit one with a clear will for victory – as part of that hypothesis, perhaps insolent, derived from our political analysis. But then something new began: we rapidly became the receptor and articulator of a wide range of popular hopes, with the responsibility that brought of building ourselves as a political force that had the capacity to rise to the challenge. At the same time, however, a campaign of harassment and persecution by the regime's forces began, of a kind that I don't think has been seen at a national level for a very long time.

The establishment was slow to react, and tried out different responses, finding out which ones had the greatest capacity to contain our progress. They adopted delaying tactics, and tried to force us into a battle of trenches and attrition, including at the personal level, in an attempt to slow down or disperse the impetus towards breaking down the existing order. Our adversaries concentrated their hopes on containment, buying themselves some time while they regrouped forces, in the hope that inertia and the traditional power structure would play into their hands, and they focused a great deal of their efforts on creating demoralisation. For us, the main goal is still to solidify the will for change; to articulate it into an alternative national project; to respond to the trust placed in us; and to keep reaching out, in alliances that cut across traditional divisions in the political arena – because the popular bloc and new majority need the support of those who still trust the traditional actors. From the beginning we've faced this challenge, this historical moment, with both humility and audacity. Humility because David only occasionally defeats Goliath. Audacity because he cannot defeat him without daring to do so.

And in the meantime, there is a set of basic tasks for assembling the raw material, the building blocks, of our project, at the educational, organisational and cultural levels. One example here is the need to remedy the dramatic absence of a flag for the construction of the national-popular. Most people with a desire for change don't have a flag that moves them – or aren't sure if they have one, or what it would be if they did. This is because of the difficulties around Spanish national identity, which was hegemonised for many decades by the right, and was built in opposition to our country's pluri-nationality.

CM: What sort of flag do you think could represent that alternative national project?

ÍE: I seriously doubt that the tricolour from the Second Spanish Republic would work for a new democratic national-popular identity. And I say this with the greatest respect for that historical experience. It's mostly a flag of nostalgia: the current crisis of the regime results from its own exhaustion; it has not resulted from a contestation of its past and founding narratives. Today the republican flag doesn't serve that purpose. One identifies with a flag because of the emotional load it carries, and its capacity to gather around itself a political will, a hope. Not because of nostalgia or its value as a piece of collectible memorabilia. The issue in Spain is whether it's possible to build a national narrative at the service of subaltern majorities that is also respectful of pluri-nationality and the right to decide – and what would be its symbolic expression. This seems to me a first-order question, not at all incidental. I think it will gradually be decided in a process of popular constitution.

CM: How do you imagine the months ahead, with all the electoral battles you'll have to face? What do you think are the main obstacles Podemos will face if it is to be able to successfully realise that project of popular constitution and democratic rupture?

ÍE: The nature, rhythm and priorities of the tasks and difficulties of the emancipatory project will be determined during the course of the dispute, by the way it develops, and by the changes in the balance of forces between the advocates of democratic rupture and those defending the restoration of the elitist order. Podemos was born out of a politico-intellectual hypothesis that allowed us to launch a risky project defying the lineal logic of force accumulation. This hypothesis, as we've already discussed, was based on an analysis of the legitimacy crisis of the traditional elite, and of the organic crisis of the institutional system – crises that had emerged not because of revolutionary contestation, but because the system wasn't capable of keeping its own promises and expectations. In that context, there were elements in the common sense of the time – still largely presided over by the world view of those above – that could be rearticulated as a different popular majority for change, one that prioritised people's needs and gave a progressive direction to feelings of exhaustion with 'the old' . Such a new discourse, needless to say, had to choose between navigating the ambivalences of its time or resigning itself to a role as an external spectator.

Podemos chose to take its hypothesis onto the immediately less gratifying ground: that of its practical confirmation. We chose to take full advantage of a deep but narrow window of opportunity, characterised by the momentary paralysis of the ruling intellectual and political sectors of the 1978 regime.

When Podemos faced its first milestone of internal construction, at Vistalegre, it took a risky political and organisational decision: to set up an electoral war machine, an agile instrument for a short cycle. This wasn't because we had a preference for rushing things, but we had an explicit desire to take full advantage of the possibilities of the moment of organic crisis and indecision from those above. We wanted to avoiding wishful thinking, but to act with audacity. That's why we chose an organisational model and strategy designed for an 'electoral blitzkrieg', a rapidly constructed electoral organisation – before the existing large political machines could reassert themselves over the general feeling of resignation. It wasn't an aesthetic or an ideological choice, but a choice informed by our aspiration for power, based on a conjunctural national analysis. It didn't exclude long-term tasks, but, equally, it didn't use them as a convenient excuse for inaction in the short term; our priorities were swiftly fixed. The main and long-term task was to build a people, but it is undeniable that this is more easily done when some parts of the institutions of the state are favourably disposed towards you. And there are times in which whole months can elapse in days.

For many months, the irruption of Podemos has disrupted all the settled plans of Spanish politics. It's caused anxiety amongst the oligarchy; it has shown how fragile some supposedly robust positions actually were; and it's precipitated processes of regeneration and renovation. It has opened a new horizon, making change imaginable, tangible, thinkable, for millions of Spaniards, in a wave of plebeian hope – 'people like me can win' – which is always a sine qua non for great change. Politics has started moving again.

The battle lines will keep changing, and it's possible that after a phase of accelerated war of position, a war of manoeuvre will follow. But conditions are already different, much more advanced, thanks to these vertiginous months: the flow of popular excitement, the growth of the organisation – with its inevitable ups and downs and specific lessons – the new confidence of those below, the rift opened in the party system and the 1978 regime. Obviously, not all the contesting forces are in place, and it is difficult to predict the next stages of the dispute between democratic change and oligarchic restoration. From now on, those working for popular sovereignty will also have to adapt, defend and advance the institutional positions they have conquered. At the same time, they'll also have to bed in the ideas, projects and people that will be able to organise a project for the country that puts its social majorities at the centre.

Building the people

Afterword to the English edition

Íñigo Errejón

This book defends a theoretical hypothesis, but also constitutes a bold experiment: the presentation of that hypothesis
through the discussion of a specific and developing political
actor – Podemos – that draws from it. It would undoubtedly
have been easier to have had a theoretical discussion with
occasional links to political realities, or, at the other end of
the spectrum, a description of a political initiative with the
theoretical references confined to a few footnotes. That would
have resulted either in a book about the 'populist hypothesis' or one about 'the Podemos phenomenon'. Instead we
decided – without really thinking too much about it – to walk
between two cliffs: abjuring both pure and abstract specula-
tion, removed from real conflicts (and their contradictions),
and a merely descriptive account of politicking and management, topical issues and the current scenario. The result is a
militant and intellectual reflection on, and assertion of: (1)
a way of understanding politics from the point of view of
hegemony theory; (2) a proposal for the reconstruction of an
emancipatory and radically democratic project, which for us
entails understanding the importance of populist passions for
transformative politics; and (3) the political force that has so
shaken up the Spanish political scene, opening up the prospect

of change towards greater social justice, popular sovereignty and the democratisation of the political system.

The book was published in Spain just before the summer of 2015 – a year after the irruption of Podemos in the European elections of 25 May 2014. During that year we had already taken decisive, and often difficult, steps towards building ourselves as a political organisation across the country, at all levels of organisation. This process had a goal: to build our organisation with great rapidity – at a pace defined by the adversary – so that by the time of the general elections in December 2015 we would be ready to constitute an alternative majority and an alternative power. That meant prioritising certain tasks over others – in particular over those of longer-term cultural construction, articulation of a popular movement, or cadre politics – in order to stage an accelerated challenge within the short electoral cycle.

At the same time, a defining feature of Podemos from the very beginning was the importance it attached to the idea of building a hegemonic project, and the struggle to create shared meanings. Two main developments came out of our project to become a hegemonic force.

On the one hand, our story transformed the political agenda in Spain, politicising the crisis and clearly indicating who was responsible for it. We built an oppositional force, a potential new popular will for national renewal. Discussions about inequality, Spain's submission to the Troika's adjustment policies, the oligarchic hijack of the institutions, and the collusion, corruption and incompetence of the old elites became commonplace on television, in public pronouncements, and in conversations in bars and workplaces. And, of all our discursive conquests, the one that most captured the Spanish collective imagination was without a doubt the term *casta*. *Casta* gave a name to a 'them' that was already visibly emerging from 2011 and the beginning of all the mobilisations – and it necessitated the construction of a new 'us'. The enormous cultural earthquake unleashed by the 15M movement – the indignados – had already established the preconditions that, in the absence of any institutional response to the increasing number of popular demands and the crisis of the political system, enabled a populist articulation that sought to bring together and unify the dissatisfactions and frustrated aspirations of a new popular identity. All the political actors, even the most conservative or reactionary, had to adapt to this change in the landscape, and modify their language, policies, and even aesthetics, if they were to avoid looking 'old' in the face of this growing, though still dispersed, desire for 'change'.

On the other hand, while superficially accepting this new atmosphere, and some of the new demands, the establishment – in a classic manoeuvre of 'passive revolution' – attempted to deprive them of their anti-oligarchic content. It partly did this through launching a massive and sustained campaign of fear against Podemos, seeking to interrupt the wave of positive response from the populace, and to stop such support from expressing itself in votes. Despite the crudeness of its arguments, this campaign should not be underestimated. If it had not been for this fearmongering and the uncertainty it generated, through associating Podemos with extremist threats from other times and places, our support and growth would have been even more extensive, especially amongst the sections of the population least disposed towards change – elderly citizens and people living in the country's interior. The traditional elites in Spain partially accepted the need for change, but at the same time committed very substantial resources to discrediting the force that had put change on the agenda.

Thus, the general election campaign took place at a difficult time for Podemos, which had experienced a year and a half of attrition in the thick of Spanish politics and been attacked on many fronts, and also had had to deal with the political dynamics of a period of rapid change, with all the contradictions that brought. Nevertheless, in spite of the atmosphere that had been orchestrated against us, our election campaign succeeded in proving wrong the analysts and pollsters who had announced the end of this anomalous phenomenon; we made a come-back, through combining good work on the political and media front with a political passion and plebeian popular enthusiasm of a kind that had been long forgotten in the tepid atmosphere of recent Spanish electoral competition. As our friend Owen Jones says in the preface to this translation, Podemos brought into play a process of popular excitement, hope and identification that brought a new sense of possibility to Spanish politics and made it possible to cut across traditional political positions.

After a surge of support as the campaign came to a close, Podemos won over 5 million votes in the election, 21 per cent of those who voted, becoming the third political force in Spain – only a point and a half behind PSOE. It came first in the Basque Country and Catalunya, and second in a number of regions that carry great political and economic weight, such as Madrid and Valencia. The election produced a set of complex and contradictory results, characteristic of a transitional time between two political eras. On the one hand, the Popular Party won the most votes in the elections, but it did not have enough parliamentary support – even with the help of Ciudadanos, a force of neoliberal regenerationism – to continue governing. Moreover, the traditional parties that typically alternate in government (PSOE and PP) only succeeded in attracting

1st over half of the vote, though, partly thanks to a system weighted towards the least populated provinces, it secured them the two top positions in parliament.

These results portray a political system in the midst of profound change, which for the moment manifests itself through two unstable equilibriums. Firstly, there is the balance of forces between, on the one hand, the most rural areas and elderly sections of the population (which are today the most solid supporters of the traditional parties) and, on the other, the more urban regions and young adult populations, especially in Madrid and the peripheral regions – where the party system has already been drastically modified, so that the town halls of the main cities in Spain (Madrid, Barcelona, Valencia, Cádiz and A Coruña) are in the hands of political change. And secondly – and connected to this balance of forces – there is the 'catastrophic draw' that characterises Spanish politics today, an impasse which means that, although democratic-popular forces have opened up a space that makes it impossible to go back to business as usual, conservative forces, while not capable of restoring the status quo, are able to veto or limit the advance of change – though not without making changes to the way the game of internal differences inside the regime is played. The key feature of this moment is that neither the forces of rupture nor those of restoration have enough strength to lead the country out of the impasse, and all the possibilities of governability involve compromises between forces of a very different nature.

Regardless of the immediate outcome of the current negotiations and the resulting government, it can't be denied that Spain is in the midst of a process of political change caused by regime crisis. This crisis involves both a crisis of legitimacy of the elites and the traditional parties, and an economic and social crisis resulting from adjustment policies, the weakening of institutions and the oligarchisation of our political system. Together with the rise of 15M, these conditions facilitated a 'populist situation' in Spain, a symbolic opposition between, on the one hand the elites and the institutional ensemble, and, on the other, a multiplicity of sectors and groups with not much in common other than their frustrated demands and their mistrust of those in power. The indignados movement expressed and framed that suffering, created an opening, and sent shock waves through the 'official country', showing the power of the 'real country'. Podemos observed those conditions and proposed the articulation of an alternative narrative, and an electoral and institutional horizon for that desire for change. Since then, we have taken steps to build – culturally, affectively, symbolically – that new political identity, and to form the nucleus of a national-popular will that is capable of turning the hopes and fears of those below into the hopes and fears of a new country, the foundations of a new historical bloc. This is an ongoing story as we write.

At the same time, the development of a national-popular and democratic project in a European Union country takes place in a set of conditions and possibilities for development that is very different from those in countries where there is also a state crisis – of monopoly over violence, territorial management or the ability of public administrations to produce certainty. We might say that the depth and speed of the processes of change in each country have been in direct proportion to the degree of its collapse or institutional decomposition, but are also related to the ability of those working for change – from an initial position of subalternity – to build a people and begin to reorder their country's political map.

Beyond the Podemos experience, which is not transposable,

and in no way offers a solution to the specifically national issues of any political process, this book seeks to make a contribution to a new perspective that brings together the best currently available efforts and reflections for the construction of a progressive, popular and emancipatory hegemony in Europe. The oligarchic advance has emptied out the terms of the post-war constitutional and social settlement; it has restricted popular sovereignty – while at the same time inflating the 'populism' ghost – and handed over many aspects of human society to predatory private powers that are not accountable to anybody. To counter this, we need to recover a sense of politics, and a passion for a democratic revolution, which is always born from 'we the people' – that is always the originary statement – construction – of a people that demands sovereignty and a new social contract. Such a revitalisation of politics requires us to think about the affective, mythical and cultural components of any identity construction, and thus to abandon a fetishism about labels and programmes and pay greater attention to metaphors and passions. It also requires us to consider the routes and agendas of a possible 'war of position' inside the state. As we say in this book, this involves imitating neoliberalism, but for the opposite ends: building new majorities so that the progressive governments of the future can institute a set of transformations and reforms such that, even when they subsequently lose power – and they all lose power eventually – their adversaries will have to govern in a very similar way to their predecessors. In other words, we need to build a new 'everydayness' that can pervade the cultural terrain, as well as public administration, the social fabric and the socio-economic model, so that limits are put on the possibilities of oligarchic regression, and we increase the potential for advancing in a popular and democratic direction.

I will end with one last point. The modest victories Podemos may have achieved in its mere two years of existence have happened because of its ability to avoid the temptation (and this has meant turning a deaf ear to well-meaning advice from right and left) of looking into manuals – old or new – in search of the exact recipe for the specific scenario for our organisation and growth. The recognition of contingency as a central fact of politics – of the need to evaluate and rethink in each moment the question of 'what to do', without falling into cynical tactical manoeuvring – is the best lesson we can extract from our short experience. I hope that in this book's previous pages, the reader has encountered, not a manual, but some clues.